PART 3
DANIEL – MALACHI

OVERVIEW

OF THE

BIBLE

BY DAVID DANN

truth
BOOKS

www.truthbooks.net

ISBN 10: 1-58427-269-4

ISBN 13: 978-158427-269-4

www.truthbooks.net

Guardian of Truth Foundation
CEI Bookstore
220 S. Marion, Athens, AL 35611
1-855-49-BOOKS or 1-855-492-6657
www.truthbooks.net

Table of Contents

Daniel 5

Hosea 12

Joel 17

Amos 22

Obadiah 28

Jonah 34

Micah 40

Nahum 46

Habakkuk 52

Zephaniah 58

Haggai 63

Zechariah 69

Malachi 76

Bibliography 82

Acknowledgements

This project would not likely have been completed without the contributions of others. I would like to thank my grandmother, Jennie Flowers, and my mother Mary Dann, for playing the roles of Lois and Eunice (2 Tim. 1:5) in cultivating within me a love for the story of the Bible. I would like to thank my father, Carl Dann, Sr., for showing me how to walk "in integrity of heart and uprightness" (1 Kings 9:4). I would like to thank Chuck Bartlett and the members of the West End church of Christ in Toronto, Canada for turning me on to the importance of teaching a survey of the books of the Bible. I would like to thank those members of the Northeast church of Christ in Clearwater, Florida whose enthusiasm for this study made it labor of love. I would also like to thank Jesse A. Flowers and Marc W. Gibson, who frequently helped in the completion of this task by listening and offering suggestions, and my brothers, Carl Dann, Jr. and James Dann for their encouragement throughout the process. And finally, I would like to thank Mike Willis, whose instruction and encouragement in writing made it possible for such a task to be undertaken.

Dedication

To my loving wife, Cynthia, whose encouraging and understanding ways enabled me to complete this project: "Many daughters have done well, but you excel them all" (Prov. 31:29). And to Olivia, Zebulon, Minnie, and Boaz who are in the process of learning the stories of the Bible: "Behold, children are a heritage from the LORD" (Psa. 127:3a).

Daniel

Introduction

Daniel is the twenty-seventh book of the Old Testament. The book of Daniel is generally recognized as the fifth of the seventeen Old Testament books of prophecy (Isaiah through Malachi), and is the fifth of the five books of the Major Prophets (Isaiah through Daniel). Daniel covers the entire period of the Babylonian captivity of Judah, from the deportation of King Jehoiakim (Dan. 1:1-2) to the reign of the Persian King, Cyrus, who allowed the Israelites to return to their homeland (10:1; cf. 2 Chron. 36:22-23). The book of Daniel consists of the story of Daniel's career in Babylon (Dan. 1-6) as well as a record of the prophetic visions of Daniel (7-12).[1] The theme of Daniel concerns the overruling authority of the one true God of heaven, who judges rebellious world empires and faithfully delivers His covenant people.

Origin of Daniel

1. Title. The book of Daniel is appropriately named for Daniel, a nobleman of Judah and prophet of God, whose prophecies and work are the subjects of the book (Dan. 1:3-6). Daniel's name means either, "God is Judge," or "God is my Judge."[2]

2. Author. The book consistently claims to contain the prophetic revelations God gave to Daniel and throughout the book Daniel speaks in the first person, indicating that he wrote what is contained in its pages (Dan. 7:1-2, 15; 8:1, 15; 9:1-2; 10:1-2; 12:5). The authorship of Daniel is confirmed through Jesus Christ, who attributes what is written in the book of Daniel to "Daniel the prophet" (Matt. 24:15; cf. Dan. 9:27; 12:11). Daniel was taken to Babylon by Nebuchadnezzar during the deportation of King Jehoiakim of Judah (Dan. 1:1-6) where he served in the court of the king of Babylon (1:18-21), and later served as a high-ranking official of the Medo-Persian Empire (6:1-2).[3] Daniel lived and prophesied during the same time period as the prophets Jeremiah (Jer. 1:1-3) and Ezekiel (Ezek. 1:1-3).

3. Date. Since the narrative of the book of Daniel extends from the deportation of King Jehoiakim (Dan. 1:1) until the third year of King Cyrus of the Medo-Persian Empire (10:1), his work covers the years from 605 B.C. to 536 B.C., spanning the entire length of the captivity of Judah in Babylon.[4] Therefore, the most likely date for the completion of the book

[1] The prophetic visions of Daniel are presented in an apocalyptic style. For a discussion of the apocalyptic writing style of the prophets, see the previous lesson.

[2] Gleason L. Archer, *A Survey of Old Testament Introduction*, 421.

[3] The deportation of Jehoiakim represents the first of the three phases of the Babylonian conquest of Judah (2 Chron. 36:5-6; 2 Kings 24:8-12; 25:1-12).

[4] Norman L. Geisler, *A Popular Survey of the Old Testament*, 284.

Notes

would be around 530 B.C., nine years after the Medo-Persian conquest of Babylon.[5] Daniel provides numerous specific chronological markers throughout the book which serve to clearly identify the time period under discussion (Dan. 1:1; 2:1; 7:1; 8:1; 9:1; 10:1).[6]

Purpose of Daniel

1. Historical purpose. The historical purpose of Daniel is to record the manner in which Daniel was used by God as part of His program of directing the affairs of the world empires which conquered and controlled His covenant people (Dan. 1:17-19; 2:24-49; 4:1-37; 5:1-29; 6:1-28). The book of Daniel records numerous prophecies of the rise and fall of various empires and kingdoms, starting with the exaltation and fall of the Babylonian Empire (Dan. 2:36-40; 5:30-31), the rise and fall of the Medo-Persian Empire (11:2), as well as the rise and fall of the Greek Empire (11:3-4), and the rise of Rome (11:40-45). Daniel's message would also encourage God's people to remain faithful and dedicated to God in a hostile, idolatrous environment while awaiting the Messiah and His kingdom by recording the manner in which Daniel and his companions remained faithful in the midst of the pressures and temptations of Babylon (Dan. 1:8; 3:1-30; 6:1-23). Additionally, the book would serve the purpose of providing comfort and encouragement to the Jews during and after their exile in Babylon by demonstrating God's control over the nations (2:20-23; 4:1-3, 34-35; 6:25-27), and pointing toward the fall of the heathen nations while revealing the future redemption of God's people (2:44-45).

2. Doctrinal purpose. Daniel is intended to teach that the superiority and glory of the true God of heaven are infinitely higher than even the most powerful nations and their idols, since He reigns supreme over the kingdoms of men (Dan. 2:20-21; 4:17). While the downfall and captivity of Judah came about as a result of the wickedness and unfaithfulness of the people (9:10-15), Daniel teaches that the future hope of God's people would be found in the mercy and faithfulness of God (9:18-19). The book also emphasizes the vital importance of trusting in God above all else, even in the face of almost certain death (3:16-18; 6:10-23). Additionally, the book of Daniel teaches that the righteous may look forward to a bright future, while the wicked may only expect misery (Dan. 12:1-3).

3. How does Daniel relate to Jesus Christ? Since Christ is the overall theme of the Bible, the book of Daniel relates to Him in some important ways. Daniel speaks clearly of the coming of the "Messiah," who would suffer the death penalty in spite of His own innocence (Dan. 9:26-27; cf.

---

[5] Gleason L. Archer, *A Survey of Old Testament Introduction*, 423.

[6] "While Daniel speaks of King Jehoiakim's deportation taking place during the third year of his reign (Dan. 1:1), Jeremiah speaks of Jehoiakim reigning in Judah during the fourth year of his reign (Jer. 25:1). This apparent discrepancy is easily explained by the fact that Jeremiah prophesied in Jerusalem, while Daniel wrote from Babylon. The correct solution, it seems to me, is to be found in the fact that Daniel here reckons the years according to the Babylonian method and Jeremiah according to the Palestinian. The year in which the king ascended the throne was designated on the Babylonian system not the first year, but 'the year of accession to the kingdom.' Hence, in mentioning the third year of Jehoiakim, Daniel has reference to the same year which Jeremiah calls the fourth" (Edward J. Young, *An Introduction to the Old Testament*, 365).

John 4:25-26; 19-1-16). Daniel also foretells the establishment of God's kingdom in the days of the Roman Empire (Dan. 2:44-45; cf. Col. 1:13-14; Rev. 1:9), and speaks of "one like the Son of Man" ascending to heaven to receive a kingdom which would extend to all nations (7:13-14; cf. Acts 1:9-11; 2:32-33; Matt. 28:18-20).

Content of Daniel

1. Daniel presents the life and work of Daniel himself. The first half of the book (Dan. 1-6) contains a considerable amount of biographical information concerning the life of Daniel, whose career spanned a period of approximately seventy years. Daniel, whose family affiliation is not specified, is introduced as being part of a certain select group of individuals taken captive to Babylon along with King Jehoiakim during Nebuchadnezzar's first campaign against Jerusalem (Dan. 1:1-6). Along with Shadrach, Meshach, and Abed-Nego, Daniel is selected to be trained to serve in the king's palace in Babylon (Dan. 1:3-7). He and his three companions quickly distinguish themselves from all others and are allowed to serve before King Nebuchadnezzar (Dan. 1:8-21). Daniel further distinguishes himself when God allows him to interpret Nebuchadnezzar's first troublesome dream (Dan. 2:1-45), is promoted to the position of ruler over the province of Babylon and chief administrator over the wise men of Babylon (2:46-49), and later interprets another troublesome dream for Nebuchadnezzar toward the end of his reign (Dan. 4:1-27). Later, when King Belshazzar's idolatrous feast is interrupted by a mysterious hand writing on the wall, Daniel is called in to interpret the writing, and in so doing proclaims the imminent fall of the Babylonian Empire to the Medes and Persians (Dan. 5:1-30).[7] However, Darius the Mede, whom the Persian conqueror, Cyrus, places over Babylon, makes Daniel a prominent governor in the early days of the Medo-Persian Empire (Dan. 6:1-3), but is pressured by Daniel's jealous colleagues to enforce a decree which Daniel violates by praying to the God of heaven (6:4-15), and, as a result, reluctantly has Daniel cast into a den of lions (6:16-17), though God preserves him from being harmed (6:18-23). Knowing the captivity of Judah to be drawing to a close, Daniel then prays to God to be merciful to His people and to restore them for His name's sake (Dan. 9:1-19). It is clear that Daniel exercised a profound influence for good upon both the Babylonian and Medo-Persian kings in whose court he served, and his influence was well-known even among the captives of Judah during his own lifetime, as evidenced by the prophet Ezekiel (Ezek. 14:14, 20; 28:3).

2. Daniel records the prophetic visions of its main character. Rather than sending him to confront the rebellious captives of Judah with God's message like Ezekiel, God communicated vital prophetic information to Daniel through various symbolic visions, which Daniel was instructed to record (Dan. 12:4). Daniel's first recorded vision comes in the first year of Belshazzar (Dan. 7:1), and consists of four great beasts who appear as a lion with eagle's wings (7:4), a bear with three ribs in its mouth (7:5), a

---

[7] It is interesting to note that Belshazzar offered Daniel the position of third ruler in the kingdom (Dan. 5:7, 16, 29), which was the highest honor he could bestow since he himself was at the time second ruler of the kingdom. He was serving as co-regent with his father, Nabonidus (Gleason L. Archer, *A Survey of Old Testament Introduction*, 427).

Notes

leopard with four wings (7:6), and a ten-horned beast with iron teeth (7:7), which give way to a vision of "one like the Son of Man" receiving a kingdom from the "Ancient of Days" (7:9-14). These represent the four world empires which would rise and fall in succession until the arrival of God's everlasting kingdom (7:17-18). Daniel's second recorded vision comes in the third year of Belshazzar (Dan. 8:1), and consists of a powerful two-horned ram which is defeated by a one-horned male goat (8:3-7), whose horn is broken and replaced by four horns (8:8-14), which is interpreted by the angel Gabriel as representing the Greek Empire's defeat of the Medo-Persian Empire (8:15-21), and the subsequent division of the Greek Empire into four parts, one of which would cause considerable harm to God's covenant people (8:9-12, 22-26).[8] Daniel's third recorded vision is presented by Gabriel in the first year of Darius the Mede (Dan. 9:1), in which seventy weeks, or sevens, represent the period of time involved in the rebuilding of the temple, the rebuilding of Jerusalem, the coming of the Messiah, the death of the Messiah, and the eventual destruction of Jerusalem and final end of the temple worship (9:24-27).[9] Daniel's fourth recorded vision comes in the third year of Cyrus (Dan. 10:1). He sees a glorious man with a thundering voice (10:4-9), and is then told that the fourth king following Cyrus to reign over the Medo-Persian Empire would fight against Greece (11:2), and eventually Greece would prevail under a mighty king whose short reign would come to an end and result in his empire being divided into four parts (11:3-4). They would then fight against one another (11:5-35), until the rise of the Roman Empire (11:36-44), which would, itself, eventually come to an end (11:45).

3. Daniel details the rise and fall of various kingdoms. While the book opens with the rise of the Babylonian Empire and the initial stages of its conquest of Judah (Dan. 1:1), the book contains a great deal of history and prophecy concerning a number of different kingdoms, including the spiritual kingdom established by Christ (7:13-14). While Daniel served in the king's palace at the height of the Babylonian Empire, Nebuchadnezzar dreamed of an image with a head of gold, chest and arms of silver, belly and thighs of bronze, and legs of iron with feet of iron mixed with clay (Dan. 2:31-35). The image was broken into pieces by a stone which became a mountain that filled the whole earth (2:34-35). Nebuchadnezzar's dream was interpreted by Daniel to represent four world empires in succession, starting with Babylon (2:36-43), while the stone which scattered the empires represents the kingdom of God which would be established during the days of the fourth world empire, and would stand forever (2:44-45).[10] Daniel provides the history of the fall of Babylon in the days

---

[8] Following the death of Alexander the Great in 323 B.C., the Greek Empire was divided into four parts, including, Macedon-Greece, Thrace-Asia Minor, the Seleucid empire (including Syria, Babylonia, and Persia), and Egypt. The "little horn" (Dan. 8:9-12) who would exalt himself against God and persecute God's people (8:23-26) corresponds to the Seleucid ruler Antiochus IV (Epiphanes), who reigned from 175-164 B.C. (*Ibid.*, 438, 440).

[9] The destruction of Jerusalem and the temple prophesied by Daniel, which brought a permanent end to sacrifices and offerings (Dan. 9:26-27; cf. Matt. 24:15-34), took place in A.D. 70 when the Roman army destroyed the city (Charles Dyer and Eugene Merrill, *Nelson's Old Testament Survey*, 716).

10 The world empires depicted in Nebuchadnezzar's dream are the Babylonian

of Belshazzar to the Medes and Persians, who would establish their rule as the second world empire of Nebuchadnezzar's dream (Dan. 5:30-31), before eventually giving way to Greece, the third empire (8:20-21; 11:2-4). The Greek Empire would eventually be overcome by a fourth empire, Rome, in whose days God's kingdom would be established (7:17-18, 27).

4. Daniel emphasizes the power and glory of God. The book of Daniel places consistent emphasis on the fact that the God of heaven is far greater and far more glorious than even the greatest earthly kings and nations. The infinite power and glory of the one true God are reinforced through Nebuchadnezzar's dream of the gold-headed image which told of the permanent superiority of God's everlasting kingdom in comparison to the kingdoms of men which pass away (Dan. 2:31-45), through God's preservation of Shadrach, Meshach, and Abed-Nego in the fiery furnace which demonstrated the superiority of God's power over idols and false gods (3:1-29), through Nebuchadnezzar's dream of the great tree which told of the superiority of God's ability to control the affairs of the kingdoms of the world and their rulers (4:1-37), through the hand which wrote on the palace wall concerning Belshazzar's demise, thereby demonstrating the superiority of God's control over the rise and fall of kingdoms (5:1-31), and through the preservation of Daniel in the lion's den, which demonstrated the superiority of God's power over plots of man's devising (6:1-28). Furthermore, the prophecies of Daniel concerning the kingdoms of the world (Dan. 7-11) would serve to continue to demonstrate the power and glory of God as the events which were accurately foretold through Daniel's visions would come to pass in the centuries following his day.[11]

Outline of Daniel

I. The Deportation of Daniel (1:1-21).
    A. The captivity of King Jehoiakim (1:1-2).
    B. The selection of the young men (1:3-7).
    C. The dedication of the young men (1:8-16).
    D. The advancement of the young men (1:17-21).

II. The Career of Daniel (2:1-6:28).
    A. Nebuchadnezzar's first dream (2:1-49).
    B. Daniel's companions in the fiery furnace (3:1-30).
    C. Nebuchadnezzar's second dream (4:1-37).
    D. Belshazzar's feast (5:1-31).
    E. Daniel in the lion's den (6:1-28).

III. The Visions of Daniel (7:1-12:13).
    A. The vision of the four beasts (7:1-28).

Empire (625-539 B.C.), the Medo-Persian Empire (539-330 B.C.), the Greek Empire (330-63 B.C.), and the Roman Empire which rose to prominence in 63 B.C. (Homer Hailey, *A Commentary On Daniel—A Prophetic Message*, 45).

[11] While Daniel lived to see the rise and fall of the Babylonian Empire, and the rise of the Medo-Persian Empire, much of his prophetic message concerning world affairs concerned events that would transpire during the period of time in between the close of the writing of the Old Testament and the beginning of the events recorded in the New Testament, regarding, in particular, the rise of the Greek Empire, its subsequent division and fall, and the rise of the Roman Empire.

B. The vision of the ram and goat (8:1-27).
C. The prayer of Daniel (9:1-19).
D. The prophecy of the Messiah (9:24-27).
E. The vision of the rise and fall of kingdoms (10:1-12:13).

Conclusion

The book of Daniel depicts the sovereign rule of God over the nations of men by looking back over the period of the Babylonian captivity of Judah and forward to the time of Christ. Daniel provides comfort for God's covenant people who had suffered at the hands of heathen nations by looking forward to the establishment of the everlasting spiritual kingdom of Christ.

Questions

1. What is the meaning of the name "Daniel," and how does the prophet's name relate to content of the book? _____

_____

2. In what way is the perspective of Daniel different from that of Ezekiel even though the two men prophesied during the same time period?

_____

_____

3. What evidence points to Daniel as the author of the book? _____

_____

_____

4. How would the following stories of Daniel and his companions encourage God's covenant people to remain faithful in spite of difficult circumstances?

a. Dan. 1:8-21. _____

b. Dan. 3:1-30. _____

c. Dan. 6:1-23. _____

5. In what ways does Daniel's prophecy of the Messiah correspond to the story of Jesus presented in the New Testament (Dan. 9:24-27)? _____

_____

_____

6. Has Daniel's vision of the "Son of Man" been fulfilled, and if so, when was it fulfilled (Dan. 7:13-14)? _____

_____

7. How did Daniel's jealous colleagues attempt to destroy him, and what does their approach say about Daniel's character (Dan. 6:1-11)? ____

_____

_____

8. Name the four world empires that are to be associated with the various parts of the image of Nebuchadnezzar's dream (Dan. 2:31-35).

a. Dan. 2:37-38. _____

b. Dan. 2:39. _____

c. Dan. 2:39. _____

d. Dan. 2:40-43. _____

9. In what time period does Nebuchadnezzar's dream place the establishment of God's kingdom (Dan. 2:44-45)? _____

_____

_____

10. How do the following episodes in the career of Daniel demonstrate the supreme power and glory of the God of heaven?

a. Dan. 2:31-45. _____

b. Dan. 3:1-29. _____

c. Dan. 4:1-37. _____

d. Dan. 5:1-31. _____

e. Dan. 6:1-28. _____

Notes

Hosea

Notes

Introduction

Hosea is the twenty-eighth book of the Old Testament. The book of Hosea is generally recognized as the sixth of the seventeen Old Testament books of prophecy (Isaiah through Malachi), and is the first of the twelve books of the Minor Prophets (Hosea through Malachi).[1] Hosea covers the period of Israelite history during which Uzziah, Jotham, Ahaz, and Hezekiah reigned as kings over the southern kingdom of Judah, while Jeroboam II reigned as king over the northern kingdom of Israel (Hos. 1:1). The theme of Hosea concerns the corruption of the northern kingdom (Hos. 4:1-13) and the prophet's attempt to persuade the people to repent and return to the God of heaven, who loves them (14:1).

Origin of Hosea

1. Title. The book of Hosea is appropriately named for Hosea the prophet of God, whose prophecies and work are the subjects of the book (Hos. 1:1). Hosea's name means, "Salvation," which is fitting in light of the fact that the book emphasizes that salvation for Israel would be found only in God (Hos. 1:7; 13:4, 10; 14:3).[2]

2. Author. The book consistently claims to contain the words that God spoke to Hosea and the words that God directed Hosea to speak to Israel (Hos. 1:1-2; 3:1). The authorship of Hosea is confirmed by the apostle Paul, who refers to the content of the book as that which God spoke through Hosea (Rom. 9:25-26; cf. Hos. 2:23; 1:10). Hosea the son of Beeri (Hos. 1:1), was apparently a citizen of the northern kingdom of Israel (7:5), whose prophetic work focused primarily on the northern kingdom, though he recognized that the Davidic dynasty of the southern kingdom of Judah was appointed by God (3:5) in contrast to the situation among the northern tribes (8:1-6). Hosea was married to an ungodly woman named Gomer (Hos. 1:2-3), and had three children, including two sons and one daughter (1:4-9). Nothing is known of Hosea other than what is stated within the book that bears his name, however, it would appear that he prophesied during the same time period as the prophets Amos and Jonah.

3 Date. Since the book states that the work of Hosea took place during the reigns of Uzziah, Jotham, Ahaz, and Hezekiah of Judah and Jeroboam the son of Joash of Israel (Hos. 1:1), the period of time involved roughly extends anywhere from 790 B.C. to 686 B.C., taking into consid-

---

[1] "It should be pointed out that the terms 'major' and 'minor' do not refer to the relative importance of their work, but rather to the length or the brevity of their books" (H.I. Hester, *The Heart of Hebrew History*, 275).

[2] Gleason L. Archer, *A Survey of Old Testament Introduction*, 356.

eration the entire time period of the reigns of those kings.[3] The prophecies recorded in the early portion of the book must have been given prior to the death of Jeroboam II, which took place in 753 B.C., since Hosea foretells the end of Jehu's dynasty, of which Jeroboam II was the last king (Hos. 1:4-5).[4] On the other hand, Hosea foretells, but does not mention the historical fulfillment of the Assyrian conquest of Israel which took place in 722 B.C (Hos. 10:5-6; 13:15-16).[5] Therefore, it seems most likely that the work of Hosea covered the period of time from around 755 B.C. to 725 B.C., and that the book was written at the end of this period of time, shortly before the fall of the northern kingdom.[6]

Purpose of Hosea

1. Historical purpose. The historical purpose of Hosea is to record the case God established against the northern kingdom with regard to unfaithfulness and corruption (Hos. 4:1-3, 11-13; 6:7-10; 7:1-4; 9:9), as well as the certainty of the punishment that would come upon God's covenant people as a direct result of their sins (5:14-15; 8:11-14; 10:8, 15; 13:7-8). The book of Hosea reveals the love of God for a sinful and rebellious people who have continually refused to be loyal to Him, as illustrated by the love of Hosea for his own unfaithful wife (Hos. 1:2; 3:1-3; 2:2-20; 11:8). Additionally, the book of Hosea records the manner in which God used the prophet to plead with His people in an attempt to persuade them to repent and return to their God so that He would extend His mercy to them (Hos. 10:12; 14:1-7). Hosea's message points forward to a time when Israel's punishment would be completed and the people would return to the true God of heaven (Hos. 1:10-11; 3:4-5; 14:8).

2. Doctrinal purpose. Hosea is intended to teach that God is loving and loyal toward His people, and He demands the same love and loyalty in return (Hos. 2:13; 6:6-7; 11:1-7). While the decline and captivity of both Israel and Judah would come about as a result of the corruption and unfaithfulness of the people (Hos. 4:6, 17-18; 5:10-12; 6:4), Hosea teaches that the future hope of God's people would be found in true repentance and a reliance upon the mercy of God (1:10-11; 2:23). The book of Hosea also emphasizes the fact that God will not accept superficial worship and shallow faith in place of true, heartfelt devotion and deep commitment to His will (Hos. 2:11; 6:1-6).

3. How does Hosea relate to Jesus Christ? Since Christ is the overall theme of the Bible, the book of Hosea relates to Him in some important ways. Hosea prophesies of a time following Israel's captivity, in the "latter days," in which the people would seek God through Christ, the "one head" who would be appointed over the people (Hos. 1:10-11), and as, "David their king" (3:4-5; cf. Luke 1:30-33). Also, Hosea's reference to God calling His Son out of Egypt is later applied by the Holy Spirit to Jesus' brief sojourn in Egypt as an infant (Hos. 11:1; cf. Matt. 2:13-15).

Content of Hosea

---

[3] Charles Dyer and Eugene Merrill, *Nelson's Old Testament Survey*, 721.

[4] Gleason L. Archer, *A Survey of Old Testament Introduction*, 357.

[5] Charles Dyer and Eugene Merrill, *Nelson's Old Testament Survey*, 722.

[6] Gleason L. Archer, *A Survey of Old Testament Introduction*, 357.

Notes

1. *Hosea uses the prophet's marriage to illustrate God's love for Israel.* The only available biographical information concerning the life of Hosea is found in the first portion of the book and has to do with the prophet's marriage to Gomer and the children she bore (Hos. 1:1-8; 3:1-3). Hosea is commanded by God to take a "wife of harlotry" as a parallel to the manner in which God has experienced the infidelity of Israel as His mate in a spiritual sense (Hos. 1:2). Hosea then marries Gomer, a daughter of the times, whose flawed character soon comes to light as she leaves him in order to commit adultery (Hos. 1:3; 3:1). However, God commands Hosea to redeem Gomer from her harlotry and take her back to himself as his wife, which he does (Hos. 3:1-2). At this point Hosea has mercy on his wife and pleads with her to remain faithful to him just as he promises to remain faithful to her (Hos. 3:3). The bitter sorrow and tragic circumstances surrounding Hosea's marriage serve to illustrate God's feelings toward Israel, who has been an adulterous wife (Hos. 2:2-3), has chased foreign lovers and played the harlot with other gods (2:7-8), has forgotten her husband (2:13), and yet would still be pursued and offered reconciliation by Him (2:14-20) because of His great mercy (2:23).

2. *Hosea exposes the sins of the northern kingdom.* Though Hosea does make reference to Judah (Hos. 4:15; 6:11; 8:14; 12:2), the focus of his message is directed toward the northern kingdom, to whom he consistently refers as "Ephraim" (4:17; 5:3, 5, 11-13; 6:47:1, 8, 11; 8:9, 11; 9:3, 13, 16; 10:11; 11:3, 8, 12; 12:1; 13:1, 12; 14:8).[7] In a general sense, the sins of the northern kingdom fall into three main categories, including a failure to acknowledge the true God (Hos. 4:4-5:15), a lack of loyal love (6:1-11:11), and a lack of faithfulness and trustworthiness (11:12-13:16). Hosea enumerates the sins of Israel as involving a lack of knowledge of God and His law (Hos. 4:6), pride (5:5), instability (6:4), worldliness (7:8), corruption (9:9), backsliding (11:7), and idolatry (13:2). In addition to these sins, Hosea charges Israel with "swearing and lying, killing and stealing and committing adultery" (Hos. 4:2), with having "transgressed the covenant" (6:7), and with robbery, murder, and lewdness (6:9). The sins of Israel would result in divine punishment in the form of the Assyrian conquest and captivity (Hos. 10:13-15; 11:5-6).

3. *Hosea focuses on the faithfulness of God.* Just as Hosea had been a faithful husband to an unfaithful wife, God had been a faithful husband to His unfaithful people (Hos. 2:2-3). However, the message of Hosea continually emphasizes the readiness and willingness of God to forgive and restore Israel should the people truly repent and turn to Him (Hos. 10:12). In the midst of the unfaithfulness of Israel, Hosea provides a constant reminder of the faithfulness of God by pointing out how He has loved and cared for Israel in the past (Hos. 11:1-3; 12:9, 13), as well as the fact that His renewed care is the only hope of Israel for the future (13:4, 9, 14). The constant love and loyalty of God toward His covenant people is expressed throughout the book along with His constant desire for them to repent so that they might obtain His mercy (Hos. 11:8; 14:1-3), even though the necessity of the punishment is readily apparent as well (8:1-3, 7).

---

[7] "Hosea called the Northern Kingdom by the name 'Ephraim' thirty-seven times. This could be because Ephraim was the strongest and most influential tribe, or because the first king of Israel, Jeroboam I, was an Ephraimite (1 Kings 11:26)" (Charles Dyer and Eugene Merrill, *Nelson's Old Testament Survey*, 723).

4. Hosea foretells the future of God's people. The immediate future of Israel is first alluded to through the names of Hosea's children, in which "Jezreel" indicates that the kingdom would be brought to an end (Hos. 1:4-5), "Lo-Ruhamah" indicates that God would no longer save them from destruction (1:6), and "Lo-Ammi" indicates that they would no longer be considered God's people due to their disobedience (1:8-9). However, the prophet also speaks of a time when Israel would be brought back to God in a renewed relationship after having rejected idolatry (Hos. 2:16-17; cf. 14:8), will enter into a new covenant that God would establish (2:18-20; cf. 14:4), and would enjoy renewed blessings and mercy (2:21-23; cf. 14:5-7). Hosea points to a future for Israel beyond the captivity in which the people would forsake idolatry and return to the true God, which would ultimately be realized through Christ, the king of the house of David (Hos. 3:4-5; cf. Acts 2:34-36), who would unite all of God's people together under His leadership (1:10-11; cf. Rom. 9:25-26).

Outline of Hosea

I. The Harlotry of Israel (1:1-3:5).
    A. The symbolism of the prophet's family (1:1-11).
    B. The unfaithfulness of God's people (2:1-13).
    C. The mercy of God toward His people (2:14-35).

II. The Case Against Israel (4:1-13:16).
    A. The sins of Israel (4:1-8:14).
    B. The judgment of God (9:1-13:16).

III. The Restoration of Israel (14:1-9).
    A. The call to repentance (14:1-3).
    B. The promise of restoration (14:4-8).
    C. The call to faithfulness (14:9).

Conclusion

The book of Hosea depicts the love and loyalty of God toward Israel as the love of a faithful husband toward an adulterous wife. Hosea reveals the punishment that Israel would suffer at the hands of the Assyrians, but also looks forward to the salvation and mercy of God which would be extended to His people through Christ.

Questions

1. Why is Hosea considered a "minor" prophet instead of a "major" prophet? _____

_____

2. What is the meaning of the name "Hosea," and how does the prophet's name relate to content of the book? _____

_____

3. Who is Hosea, and what evidence exists to show that he wrote the book? _____

_____

Notes

4. According to Hosea, why should Israel have been faithful and loyal to God (Hos. 11:1-4)? _____

_____

_____

5. How do the following passages of Hosea relate to Jesus Christ?

a. Hos. 1:10-11. _____

b. Hos. 3:4-5. _____

c. Hos. 11:1. _____

6. How does Hosea's marriage illustrate God's relationship with Israel (Hos. 1:2-3; 2:13; 3:1-5)? _____

_____

7. Describe the sins of Israel which are discussed in the following passages:

a. Hos. 4:6. _____

b. Hos. 5:5. _____

c. Hos. 6:4. _____

d. Hos. 7:8. _____

e. Hos. 9:9. _____

f. Hos. 11:7. _____

g. Hos. 13:2. _____

8. Why should Israel continue to hope and trust in God even in the face of the Assyrian conquest and captivity (Hos. 13:4, 9, 14)? _____

_____

9. How do the names of Hosea's children indicate what God had planned for Israel?

a. Jezreel (Hos. 1:4-5). _____

b. Lo-Ruhama (Hos. 1:6). _____

c. Lo-Ammi (Hos. 1:8-9). _____

10. What aspects of Israel's restoration following the captivity are emphasized in the following passages?

a. Hos. 2:16-17. _____

b. Hos. 2:18-20. _____

c. Hos. 2:21-23. _____

Joel

Introduction

Joel is the twenty-ninth book of the Old Testament. The book of Joel is generally recognized as the seventh of the seventeen Old Testament books of prophecy (Isaiah through Malachi), and is the second of the twelve books of the Minor Prophets (Hosea through Malachi). The theme of Joel is centered on a solemn warning of the divine judgment God would bring upon His people in "the day of the Lord" (Joel 1:15), which is accompanied by the prophet's call for the people to turn to God in true repentance so that they might partake of His mercy (2:12-13).

Origin of Joel

1. Title. The book of Joel is appropriately named for Joel the prophet of God, whose prophecies make up the content of the book (Joel 1:1). Joel's name means, "Jehovah is God," which is fitting in light of the fact that the book emphasizes that God would prove to His people that He is the true God of heaven (Joel 2:27; 3:17).[1]

2. Author. The opening statement of the book presents the claim that it contains the words that God spoke to Joel, the son of Pethuel (Joel 1:1). The authorship of Joel is confirmed by the apostle Peter, who refers to the content of the book as that which "was spoken by the prophet Joel" (Acts 2:16-21; cf. Joel 2:28-32). Joel the son of Pethuel (Joel 1:1), was apparently a citizen of the southern kingdom of Judah whose prophetic work focused primarily on the southern kingdom and the city of Jerusalem (2:1, 15), and on the priests who ministered at the temple in Jerusalem (1:9, 13-14; 2:17), while looking forward to a time when God would alleviate the suffering of Judah and Jerusalem (3:1, 6). Nothing is known of Joel other than what is stated within the book that bears his name.

3. Date. While Joel's exclusive focus on the southern kingdom of Judah would place the time of his work in the period of the Divided Kingdom, the book lacks any mention of a king of Judah with whom its time period may be associated. Since Joel does not mention a king of Judah, but instead directs his message toward the elders and priests (Joel 1:2-3, 13-14), his work would seem to naturally coincide with the period of time during which Judah made the transition from being ruled by the murderous queen Athaliah to the reign of her young grandson Joash, whose affairs were directed by Jehoiada the priest until he came of age (2 Kings 11:1-12:2). Another line of evidence pointing to this time period is the focus on enemies of Israel such as Tyre and Sidon, the Philistines, the Egyptians, and the Edomites (Joel 3:4, 19), rather than the Assyrians and Babylonians, who became a problem for Judah in a later time period.[2] Therefore,

Notes

---

[1] H. I. Hester, *The Heart of Hebrew History*, 278.

[2] "At no time after the reign of Joash was the kingdom of Judah faced by this

it seems most likely that the work of Joel covered the time period around 835-830 B.C., and that the book was written around 830 B.C.[3]

Purpose of Joel

1. Historical purpose. The historical purpose of Joel is to record how God warned Judah of His coming judgment against His people for their sins (Joel 2:1-11), as well as to record the exhortation of Joel for God's people to avoid this terrible judgment by repenting of their sins (2:12-14). The book of Joel speaks of the devastation brought on by a recent plague of locusts (Joel 1:1-20), and points toward an even worse punishment that would come upon God's covenant people should they refuse to repent and return to Him (2:15-17). Additionally, the book of Joel records the manner in which God would judge the surrounding nations (3:1-17), and eventually restore and bless Judah (2:18-27; 3:18-21), ultimately pointing toward the pouring out of the Spirit of God in connection with the salvation and deliverance of a righteous remnant (2:28-32).

2. Doctrinal purpose. Joel is intended to teach that it is well within God's power to both judge (Joel 1:15-18) and bless (2:18-19) His people in response to either their wickedness or faithfulness. The book also teaches that even God's covenant people need to be continually reminded that He is the true and living God and is superior to all others (Joel 2:27; 3:17). Additionally, the book of Joel emphasizes the need for true repentance from the heart, rather than a mere outward show of sorrow, on the part of those who seek reconciliation with God (Joel 2:12-13).

3. How does Joel relate to Jesus Christ? Since Christ is the overall theme of the Bible, the book of Joel relates to Him in some important ways. Joel prophesies of a time when God's Spirit would be poured out, signaling the start of a new era in which salvation would be available for all who call upon the name of the Lord (Joel 2:28-32), which would be fulfilled in the Holy Spirit's arrival on the Day of Pentecost following the resurrection of Christ (Acts 2:1-4, 14-21), at which time the availability of forgiveness of sins through Christ would be announced (2:38-41).

Content of Joel

1. Joel presents a plague of locusts. The book opens by indicating that an unusually devastating infestation of locusts has swept through the land of Judah leaving misery in its wake (Joel 1:2-12). As Joel points out, the swarms of locusts have come in waves and have eaten everything in their path (Joel 1:4), have stripped the vines and fruit trees (1:7), have devoured anything that may be offered to God (1:9), and have taken away the harvest of the field (1:10-11). Though the locust plague would cause the elders (Joel 1:2), farmers (1:11), and priests of Judah (1:9, 13) to lament and mourn the devastation, the locusts actually signify an even harsher judgment of God in the form of an invasion by a powerful and ruthless army (2:1-11). Following the locust plague and in view of the coming military invasion, Joel calls upon the people of Judah to repent and cast their hopes upon the mercy of

---

particular assortment of enemies" (Gleason L. Archer, *A Survey of Old Testament Introduction*, 339).

[3] Charles Dyer and Eugene Merrill, *Nelson's Old Testament Survey*, 737-738.

God (Joel 2:12-17), with the promise that God would have pity on His people and their land (2:18), would deliver them from destruction (2:19-20), and would restore their blessings (2:21-26), thereby proving His power and deity (2:27).

2. *Joel contains the curses of the covenant.* The Law of Moses warned of various specific curses that would befall the Israelites should they rebel against God after taking possession of the Promised Land (Deut. 28:15-68). The judgments of God described in the book of Joel parallel the curses of disobedience previously recorded by Moses. It is evident that in the days of Joel the covenant people of God suffered the very curses of which the law warned, including the plague of locusts consuming the produce of the field and the trees (cf. Joel 1:4, 7; Deut. 28:38, 42), the destruction of the produce of the vineyards (cf. Joel 1:11-12; Deut. 28:39), the failure of the olive trees (cf. Joel 1:10; Deut. 28:40), the extreme drought brought on by lack of rain (cf. Joel 1:17-20; Deut. 28:24), the invasion of the land by a destroying army (cf. Joel 2:1-11; Deut. 28:25, 33, 47-51), and the people of God becoming a reproach among the nations (cf. Joel 2:17, 19; Deut. 28:37). As Joel instructs, the only hope of restoration lay in the willingness of the people to turn to God in true repentance (cf. Joel 2:12-17; Deut. 30:1-10).

3. *Joel emphasizes the day of the Lord.* Though the theme of the "day of the Lord" is found throughout the prophet's message (Joel 1:15; 2:1, 11, 31; 3:14), its precise meaning varies within the book. When first introduced, "day of the Lord" is presented as a day of destruction and punishment (Joel 1:15) that God has brought upon His rebellious people through the devastating plague of locusts (1:4-12) and the accompanying drought (1:16-20). Next, "day of the Lord" is presented as a "day of darkness and gloominess" as it reflects the divine punishment that awaits Judah by means of an invading army (Joel 2:1-2), representing a day that can scarcely be endured (2:11). The meaning of the "day of the Lord" then shifts to reflect a solemn day of deliverance as the prophet's message turns toward the time when God would pour out His Spirit on man and make salvation available to all who call upon Him (2:28-32). Finally, the prophet speaks of the "day of the Lord" in describing God's condemnation of the wicked and vindication of the righteous of His people (Joel 3:14-16). In its various manifestations, it is obvious that "day of the Lord" is employed by Joel in order to refer to an event in which God intervenes to defeat evil, judge the wicked, or to provide deliverance for the faithful.

4. *Joel delivers a message of salvation.* The deliverance and salvation of God presented in the book of Joel depends on the grace and mercy of God on the one hand (Joel 2:18; 3:21), and on the repentance and obedience of man on the other (1:13-14; 2:12-13). Joel emphasizes the basic truth that the just judgment of God condemns all sinners (Joel 3:9-15), while the compassionate mercy of God provides salvation for those who repent and obey His will (2:12-13; 3:16-17, 21). The most striking message of salvation presented in the book of Joel concerns the time at which God would pour out His Spirit on man (Joel 2:28-31), signaling the arrival of a deliverance so great that it may truly be said that "whoever calls on the name of the Lord shall be saved" (2:32). The message of salvation

Notes

proclaimed by the prophet Joel would ultimately find fulfillment in the new covenant of Jesus Christ (Acts 2:21, 36-38; Rom. 10:12-13).[4]

Outline of Joel

I. Judgment in the Day of the Lord (1:1-2:17).
   A. The present devastation by the locust plague (1:1-20).
   B. The future devastation by the locust-like army (2:1-11).
   C. The need for true repentance (2:12-17).

II. Deliverance in the Day of the Lord (2:18-3:21).
   A. The promise of present restoration (2:18-27).
   B. The promise of future restoration (2:28-32).
   C. The judgment of the nations (3:1-17).
   D. The blessings of the faithful (3:18-21).

Conclusion

The book of Joel combines the just judgment of God against wickedness with the compassionate mercy of God toward those who wholeheartedly turn to Him. Joel emphasizes the certainty of God's judgment against the ungodly, while at the same time looking forward to the gracious salvation He would make available to all men through Christ.

Questions

1. What is the meaning of the name "Joel," and how does the prophet's name relate to content of the book (Joel 2:27; 3:17)? _____

_____

2. Who is Joel, and what evidence exists to show that he wrote the book?

_____

_____

3. How does the mention of certain nations as enemies of Israel provide evidence as to the time period of Joel's prophecy (Joel. 3:4, 19)? ____

_____

4. According to the book of Joel, what is the difference between true repentance and superficial repentance (Joel. 2:12-13)? _____

_____

5. What is the connection between Joel's prophecy of the pouring out of the Holy Spirit and salvation through Jesus Christ (Joel 2:28-32)? ___

_____

_____

---

[4] The New Testament makes it clear that in order for one to "call upon the name of the Lord" and "be saved" one must sincerely comply with the Lord's terms for forgiveness of sins as prescribed by his apostles (Acts 2:36-41; Rom. 6:17-18; Mark 16:15-16).

6. How do the following passages of Joel describe the effects of the locust plague?

a. Joel 1:4. _____

b. Joel 1:7. _____

c. Joel 1:9. _____

d. Joel 1:10-11. _____

7. What kind of an impact should God's deliverance of Judah have had on His people (Joel 2:27)? _____

_____

8. How does the punishment of Judah described in the book of Joel parallel the curses of the covenant?

a. Joel 1:4, 7; Deut. 28:38, 42. _____

_____

b. Joel 1:11-12; Deut. 28:39. _____

_____

c. Joel 1:10; Deut. 28:40. _____

_____

d. Joel 1:17-20; Deut. 28:24. _____

_____

e. Joel 2:1-11; Deut. 28:25, 33, 47-51. _____

_____

f. Joel 2:17, 19; Deut. 28:37. _____

_____

9. What does the "day of the Lord" depict in the following passages?

a. Joel 1:15. _____

b. Joel 2:1, 11. _____

c. Joel 2:31-32. _____

d. Joel 3:12-16. _____

10. How does Joel emphasize the fact that God is both just and merciful (Joel 3:12-16)? _____

_____

Amos

Introduction

Amos is the thirtieth book of the Old Testament. The book of Amos is generally recognized as the eighth of the seventeen Old Testament books of prophecy (Isaiah through Malachi), and is the third of the twelve books of the Minor Prophets (Hosea through Malachi). The theme of Amos concerns God's faithfulness to His covenant (Amos 3:1-2), coupled with the fact that He would hold Israel accountable for their failure to fulfill their obligations to the covenant (3:13-4:3). Amos stresses the failure of God's people in general, and the northern kingdom of Israel in particular, to faithfully and wholeheartedly comply with the Law of Moses (Amos 2:4-8; 8:1-8).

Origin of Amos

1. Title. The book of Amos is appropriately named for Amos the prophet of God, whose prophecies make up the content of the book (Amos 1:1). The prophet's name most likely means, "burden-bearer," which is fitting in light of the fact that God laid upon Amos the weighty responsibility of presenting His powerful message to Israel (Amos 7:14-15).[1]

2. Author. The opening statement of the book presents the claim that it contains the words that God spoke to Amos (Amos 1:1), who, although a citizen of the southern kingdom, was sent by God to prophesy to the northern kingdom (7:15). Amos is described as a "herdsman of Tekoa" (Amos 1:1), a town of Judah situated five miles southeast of Bethlehem and twelve miles south of Jerusalem.[2, 3] In addition to his occupation as a "herdsman," or one who "followed the flock" (Amos 7:14-15), Amos also describes himself as "a tender of sycamore fruit" (7:14), who was called by God to prophesy even though he did not consider himself to be a prophet, nor "a son of a prophet" (7:14).[4] Nothing is known of Amos other than what is stated within the book that bears his name, however, it would appear that he prophesied during the same time period as the prophets Hosea and Jonah.

3. Date. The words of Amos which are recorded in the book are stated to have been delivered by Amos to Israel "in the days of Uzziah king of Judah, and in the days of Jeroboam, the son of Joash, king of Israel, two

---

[1] Gleason L. Archer, *A Survey of Old Testament Introduction*, 351.

[2] H. I. Hester, *The Heart of Hebrew History*, 281.

[3] Gleason L. Archer, *A Survey of Old Testament Introduction*, 352.

[4] "The terms 'son of a prophet' and 'sons of the prophets' were used at that time to identify a group of disciples or followers who were attached to a prophet (2 Kings 2:3; 4:1, 38; 5:22)" (Charles Dyer and Eugene Merrill, *Nelson's Old Testament Survey*, 746).

years before the earthquake" (Amos 1:1). Since Uzziah reigned from 790-739 B.C. and Jeroboam II reigned from 793-753 B.C., Amos must have completed his work at some point during this time period.[5] Amos' reference to the earthquake (Amos 1:1) indicates that the book was written at least two years after he completed his work; however, even though it was powerful enough to leave a lasting impression (cf. Zech. 14:5), the exact date of the earthquake is unknown.[6] A good estimate for the work of Amos is that his ministry to Israel took place around 755 B.C.[7]

Purpose of Amos

1. Historical purpose. The historical purpose of Amos is to record the manner in which God used Amos to warn Israel of impending judgment and inescapable punishment (Amos 2:6-16; 3:9-15; 4:12; 5:3, 18-20; 6:14; 8:2; 9:1), to issue a call to repentance (5:4-15), and to a lesser extent, to warn Judah to repent and observe the law of God (2:4-5; 6:1-8). The book of Amos describes the sinfulness of the northern kingdom as including extreme greed and materialism (Amos 2:6), sexual immorality (2:7), idolatry (2:8), disregard for the law of Moses (2:11-12), oppression of the poor (4:1), and an overall rejection of justice and righteousness (5:6-7, 12). Additionally, the book of Amos records God's condemnation of the surrounding nations (Amos 1:3-2:3), as well as His promise of future blessings for His people, including those Gentiles who would come to Him (9:11-15).

2. Doctrinal purpose. Amos is intended to teach that God expects to see justice on the part of His people in relation to their dealings with one another, and righteousness in relation to their dealings with Him (Amos 5:7, 12, 24; 6:12), rather than violence (3:10; 5:11), and corrupted worship (4:4-5; 5:25-27). The book also teaches that, even in the midst of extreme wickedness, there exists the possibility of repentance (Amos 5:4-6, 14), as well as the perseverance of a faithful remnant (5:15; 9:8). Additionally, the book of Amos teaches that, though God is longsuffering, sinners must accept correction while there is still time (Amos 4:6-11; 5:10), because the time will soon arrive when man will be held accountable for his sins (4:12; 5:18-20, 24).

3. How does Amos relate to Jesus Christ? Since Christ is the overall theme of the Bible, the book of Amos relates to Him in some important ways. Amos prophesies of a time when God would "raise up the tabernacle of David" (Amos 9:11), welcome the inclusion of the Gentiles as part of His people (9:12), and overwhelm His people with blessings (9:13-15), all of which would be fulfilled in Christ (Luke 1:30-33; Acts 15:6-17; Eph. 1:3).

Content of Amos

1. Amos includes the message and work of Amos the prophet. While the book of Amos is not biographical in nature, it does state that Amos was an ordinary shepherd and farmer whom God called into service as a prophet to go and speak out against the sins of Israel (Amos 7:14-15). The book records the manner in which Amos warned Israel of the certain doom that God would bring upon the nation for its sins (Amos 4:12; 8:2),

[5] Gleason L. Archer, *A Survey of Old Testament Introduction*, 353.

[6] *Ibid.*, 353.

[7] Norman L. Geisler, *A Popular Survey of the Old Testament*, 237.

including the impending prospect of captivity (5:27; 6:14; 7:17; 9:8-10). The prophet's message to God's people was one which exposed their sins (Amos 2:6-8; 5:12; 8:5-6), condemned their corrupt religion which mixed idolatry with the worship of the God of heaven (4:4-5; 5:25-27), rebuked their stubbornness (4:6-11) and complacency (6:1-8), and called upon them to repent and "seek the Lord" (5:4, 6, 14-15). The message of Amos was so stern that Amaziah, the priest of Bethel, complained that it was unbearable (Amos 7:10-11) and commanded him to cease prophesying and depart from the northern kingdom (7:12-13), only to receive an even more severe rebuke from the Lord (7:17). However, Amos ended his message in a hopeful manner by expressing the promise of God that Israel would not entirely perish from the earth (Amos 9:8), and that His people would be blessed in the future (9:11-15).

2. Amos consists of three sections. The book of Amos may be divided into three distinct sections, including a section containing eight oracles, or proclamations (Amos 1-2), a section containing three sermons (3-6), and a section containing six visions of judgment and restoration (7-9). The first section of the book features eight proclamations of God's judgment on various sinful nations beginning with those enemy nations which bordered Israel and Judah, including Syria (Amos 1:3-5), Philistia (1:6-8), Phoenicia (1:9-10), Edom (1:11-12), Ammon (1:13-15), and Moab (2:1-3), and finally dealing with both Judah (2:4-5), and Israel (2:6-16). The second section of the book features three sermons which begin with the exhortation to "Hear this word" (Amos 3:1; 4:1; 5:1), and address sin as the reason for God's judgment (3:1-15), destruction as the result of God's judgment (4:1-15), and the need for true repentance in view of the certainty of God's judgment (5:1-6:14). The third section of the book features six visions, of which the first five, including the locusts (7:1-3), the fire (7:4-6), the plumb line (7:7-9), the summer fruit (8:1-14), and the vision of God at the altar (9:1-10) depict God's judgment, while the sixth provides a view of restoration and a hopeful future for the faithful remnant of God's people (9:11-15).

3. Amos reflects the Law of Moses. In reviewing the various ways in which God's people had sinned, Amos points out numerous areas wherein they had specifically violated the covenant that God made with them. Amos emphasizes the fact that Israel repeatedly transgressed God's covenant by engaging in religious prostitution (Amos 2:7; cf. Deut. 23:17-18), keeping garments taken in a pledge overnight (Amos 2:8; cf. Exod. 22:26; Deut. 24:12-13), defiling the Nazirites (Amos 2:11-12; cf. Num. 6:1-21), offering sacrifices with leaven (Amos 4:5; cf. Lev. 2:11; 7:12), treating the poor unjustly (Amos 5:11-12; cf. Lev. 19:15), and engaging in dishonest business practices (Amos 8:5; cf. Lev. 19:35-36). The judgment which God pronounced against His people through Amos was made necessary by their complete disregard for His law (Amos 2:4).

4. Amos features vivid imagery. The words of Amos paint pictures of memorable images, both of the sins of the people, and the judgment of God. The imagery of Israel's sin employed by Amos includes the picture of greedy Israelites selling the poor for a pair of sandals (Amos 2:6), the picture of God being weighed down by the sins of Israel just as a cart would be weighed down by heavy sheaves of grain (2:13), the picture of the people of Israel trampling the poor (5:11), and the picture of the people of Judah reclining in spiritual complacency on beds of ivory (6:1-4). The imagery of God's judgment against Israel employed by Amos includes the picture of destruction so severe that it is compared to what is left of an animal after a lion tears it to pieces (Amos 3:12), the picture of God cutting off the horns of the idolatrous altar of Bethel (2:14), the picture of the sinful women of Israel as cows who will be led away with fishhooks (4:1-3), the picture of God's judgment being as inescapable as a man trying to escape a lion only to be attacked by a bear or bitten by a snake (5:19), the picture of God's judgment running down like a mighty stream of water (5:24), the picture of the land of Israel trembling and heaving like a river (8:8), and the picture of God sifting and scattering Israel throughout the nations like grain (9:9). On the other hand, future spiritual blessings which God would bestow upon the faithful are pictured in terms of harvesting an overwhelming abundance of food (Amos 9:13).

Outline of Amos

I. The Proclamations of Judgment on the Nations (1:1-2:16).
    A. Introduction (1:1-2).
    B. Judgment on Syria (1:3-5).
    C. Judgment on Philistia (1:6-8).
    D. Judgment on Phoenicia (1:9-10).
    E. Judgment on Edom (1:11-12).
    F. Judgment on Ammon (1:13-15).
    G. Judgment on Moab (2:1-3).
    H. Judgment on Judah (2:4-5).
    I. Judgment on Israel (2:6-16).

II. The Messages of Judgment on Israel (3:1-6:14).
    A. The punishment of Israel (3:1-15).
    B. The sins of Israel (4:1-13).
    C. The call to repentance (5:1-15).
    D. The destruction of Israel (5:16-27).
    E. The complacency of God's people (6:1-14).

III. The Visions of Judgment on Israel (7:1-9:1-10).
    A. The visions of the locusts, the fire, and the plumb line (7:1-17).
    B. The vision of the basket of summer fruit (8:1-14).
    C. The vision of God at the altar (9:1-10).

IV. The Hope of Israel (9:11-15).
    A. The restoration of the tabernacle of David (9:11-12).
    B. The blessings of the faithful (9:13-15).

Conclusion

The book of Amos presents God's case against Israel along with the certainty of his judgment against Israel and the surrounding nations. Amos emphasizes the manner in which Israel had broken God's covenant and the punishment that would follow, while also looking forward to the future blessings that would be made available to both Israelite and Gentile alike through Christ.

Notes

Questions

1. What is the meaning of the name "Amos," and how does the prophet's name relate to content of the book (Amos 7:14-15)? _____

   _____

2. What was Amos' background, and why is it ironic that he was sent by God to prophesy against the northern kingdom (Amos 1:1; 7:14-15)?

   _____

   _____

3. How had Israel neglected both justice and righteousness (Amos 5:12; 4:4-5)? _____

   _____

4. Why did God pronounce judgment on the following nations?

   a. Syria (Amos 1:3). _____

   b. Philistia (Amos 1:6). _____

   c. Phoenicia (Amos 1:9). _____

   d. Edom (Amos 1:11). _____

   e. Ammon (Amos 1:13). _____

   f. Moab (Amos 2:1). _____

5. How had God tried to bring Israel to repentance (Amos 4:6-11)? ____

   _____

6. What is the connection between the following items of Amos' prophecy of the future of God's people and Jesus Christ?

   a. The tabernacle of David (Amos 9:11). _____

   _____

   b. The Gentiles (Amos 9:12). _____

   c. The blessings (Amos 9:13-15). _____

7. Why did Amaziah complain about Amos' message, and what was the outcome of his complaint (Amos 7:10-17)? _____

   _____

8. Into what sections may the book of Amos be divided?

   a. Amos 1-2. _____

   b. Amos 3-6. _____

   c. Amos 7-9. _____

9. According to Amos, how had Israel violated the Law of Moses?

a. Amos 2:7; cf. Deut. 23:17-18. _____

_____

b. Amos 2:8; cf. Exod. 22:26. _____

c. Amos 2:11-12; cf. Num. 6:1-21. _____

_____

d. Amos 4:5; cf. Lev. 2:11. _____

_____

e. Amos 5:11-12; cf. Lev. 19:15. _____

_____

f. Amos 8:5; cf. Lev. 19:35-36. _____

_____

10. What does Amos emphasize through the imagery used in the following passages?

a. Amos 2:13. _____

b. Amos 3:12. _____

c. Amos 9:13. _____

Notes

Obadiah

Notes

Introduction

Obadiah is the thirty-first book of the Old Testament. The book of Obadiah is generally recognized as the ninth of the seventeen Old Testament books of prophecy (Isaiah through Malachi), and is the fourth of the twelve books of the Minor Prophets (Hosea through Malachi). The theme of Obadiah concerns the severe judgment which God would visit upon Edom for its cruel and prideful attitude toward God's covenant people (Obad. 1-4, 10), while at the same time presenting a message of hope and deliverance to Judah (17). While the message of Obadiah is primarily about Edom, it was actually delivered to Judah (Obad. 11, 17, 21). The book of Obadiah is the shortest book of the Old Testament.

Origin of Obadiah

1. Title. The book of Obadiah is appropriately named for Obadiah the prophet of God, whose prophecies make up the content of the book (Obad. 1). The prophet's name means, "Servant of Jehovah," which serves as a contrast against the pride and ungodliness of Edom (Obad. 3).[1]

2. Author. The opening statement of the book presents the claim that it contains a record of the vision which God revealed to Obadiah (Obad. 1), who was apparently a citizen of the southern kingdom of Judah (11-12). Although numerous individuals named Obadiah are mentioned throughout the Old Testament (1 Kings 18:3-16; 1 Chron. 3:21; 7:3; 9:16; 12:9; 27:19; 2 Chron. 17:7; 34:12; Ezra 8:9; Neh. 10:5; 12:25), there is no reason to identify the author of this book with any of them. Nothing is known of Obadiah outside of the book that bears his name.

3. Date. Due to its lack of specific historical markers and the obscurity of the prophet himself, the book of Obadiah is widely considered to be the most difficult of all of the books of the prophets when it comes to the matter of assigning a precise date to its message.[2] Scholars remain divided as to whether the book should be dated during the time of king Jehoram of Judah (ca. 848-841 B.C.), shortly after the Babylonian conquest of Judah (ca. 586 B.C.), or somewhere in between those two periods of time.[3] While the book does describe a particular destruction of Jerusalem at the hands of her enemies, as well as the captivity of some of the inhabitants of Judah (Obad. 12-13), the destruction described by Obadiah does not appear to be the complete and final destruction at the hands of

---

[1] H. I. Hester, *The Heart of Hebrew History*, 292.

[2] Gleason L. Archer, *A Survey of Old Testament Introduction*, 332.

[3] Norman L. Geisler, *A Popular Survey of the Old Testament*, 251-252.

the Babylonians that took place in 586 B.C. (cf. Jer. 52:1-30).[4] Evidence favoring the earlier date includes the following: (a) the events described by Obadaiah (Obad. 11-14) seem to correspond well with the revolt of the Edomites (2 Kings 8:20-22) and the invasion and plundering of Jerusalem by the Philistines and Arabians that took place during the reign of Jehoram (2 Chron. 21:8-10, 16-17); (b) Judah's enemies as described in the book are the Edomites and Philistines (Obad. 19), rather than Babylon; (c) Obadiah describes the foreigners who have invaded Jerusalem as casting lots for the plunder of the city (Obad. 11), rather than the city becoming the property of Babylon; (d) the prophecy of Jeremiah concerning Edom (cf. Jer. 49:7-22; Obad. 1-9, 15-16) appears to be a later prophecy that reiterates those things that had earlier been prophesied by Obadiah; (e) it is possible that the prophet Joel, prophesying around 830 B.C., makes reference to what had previously been stated by Obadiah (cf. Joel 2:32; Obad. 17); and (f) Obadiah speaks of the exiles of Judah being taken to Sepharad (Obad. 20), rather than to Babylon.[5] Therefore, it seems most likely that Obadiah describes events that took place during the reign of king Jehoram (848-841 B.C.), and that the book was written around this time, possibly in 845 B.C.[6]

Purpose of Obadiah

1. *Historical purpose.* The historical purpose of Obadiah is to record the manner in which God used Obadiah to announce the destruction that He would bring upon Edom due to its prideful and hateful attitude toward Judah (Obad. 1-9). The book of Obadiah describes the haughty attitude of Edom (Obad. 3), as well as Edom's mistreatment of Judah (10-14) at a time when Jerusalem was plundered by enemies (11). Additionally, the book of Obadiah would offer comfort to Judah in that, while the enemies of God's people would be punished (Obad. 15-16), God would also provide deliverance for His own people (17-21).

2. *Doctrinal purpose.* Obadiah is intended to teach that pride and self-exaltation, as seen in the case of Edom, will prevent man from being acceptable to God, and will lead only to destruction (Obad. 3-4; cf. 1 Pet. 5:5-6; Prov. 16:18; 1 Cor. 10:12). The book also teaches that God will judge those who rejoice in the calamity of others (Obad. 12-13), and will view those who share in the spoils of wickedness and those who refuse to oppose wickedness the same as those originally responsible for committing the wickedness (11; cf. 2 John 9-11). Additionally, the book of Obadiah teaches that those whose dealings with others are characterized by cruelty, bitterness, and hatred will certainly face the wrath of God in return

---

[4] Evidence in favor of the later date for the prophecy of Obadiah includes the fact that Edom rejoiced over the Babylonian conquest of Judah (Psa. 137:7; Lam. 4:21-22) and added to Judah's suffering at that time (Ezek. 25:12-14; 35:1-15; 36:4-5).

[5] "The most likely identification connects Sepharad with a district referred to as Shaparda in southwestern Media mentioned in an inscription of King Sargon of Assyria. It is well known that Sargon deported some of the ten tribes to the 'cities of the Medes' (see 2 Kings 18:11). Therefore this locality would have been very appropriate to mention in Obadiah's prediction" (Gleason L. Archer, *A Survey of Old Testament Introduction*, 336).

[6] *Ibid.*, 333.

for their ungodly behavior (Obad. 10, 15-16), while deliverance will be provided for the righteous (17, 21).

3. How does Obadiah relate to Jesus Christ? Since Christ is the overall theme of the Bible, the book of Obadiah relates to Him in some important ways. Obadiah prophesies of a time when God would provide salvation in Mount Zion, or Jerusalem (Obad. 17, 21), which would ultimately be fulfilled when the message of salvation in Christ would be introduced in, and sent forth from, Jerusalem (cf. Luke 24:26-29; Acts 1:8). Obadiah also speaks of a time when the kingdom would belong to the Lord (Obad. 21), thereby pointing forward to the spiritual kingdom of Christ which is made up of the saved (Mark 9:1; Col. 1:13-14).

Content of Obadiah

1. Obadiah provides a description of Edom. In presenting a prophetic message "concerning Edom" (Obad. 1), the book of Obadiah describes the territory and terrain occupied by the Edomites. The country of Edom bordered Judah on the south and was located directly south of the Dead Sea.[7] Obadiah refers to the Edomites as those "who dwell in the clefts of the rock" (Obad. 3) in order to emphasize the rugged and rocky terrain of the country, and also speaks of Edom as the nation "whose habitation is high" (3) and speaks of the Edomites as a people occupying a mountainous territory (8-9, 19). The book ties the prideful attitude of Edom to the nation's feeling of invincibility derived from occupying elevated strongholds that would not be easily attacked in the midst of difficult terrain (Obad. 3-4). However, even a nation as well-situated for defense as Edom would not be able to defend itself against the judgment of the God of heaven (Obad. 2-9).

2. Obadiah condemns the sins of Edom. The prophet sets forth God's case against Edom, justifying the divine battle that He will wage against that wicked nation (Obad. 1). Aside from its obvious prideful attitude (Obad. 3-4), Obadiah pronounces condemnation on Edom principally due to what is described as Edom's "violence" against Judah (10). The sins which Edom committed against Judah are presented by the prophet as including: (a) the fact that Edom "stood on the other side" and refused to help when Judah was being attacked and invaded by enemies, thereby effectively becoming "as one of" Judah's attackers (Obad. 11); (b) the fact that Edom gazed upon and rejoiced over Judah's troubles as Jerusalem was being plundered (12); (c) the fact that Edom "entered the gate" of Jerusalem and took advantage of the opportunity to seize the wealth of its citizens (13); and (d) the fact that Edom "stood at the crossroads" as the inhabitants of Jerusalem fled and either killed or handed over to the enemy those who were trying to escape (14). For this cruel behavior Edom would be severely punished by God (Obad. 15).

3. Obadiah pronounces judgment on Edom. Much of the book of Obadiah consists of a sweeping denunciation of Edom and a promise of certain destruction from the hand of God upon the wicked nation. The book opens with the call for divine battle against Edom (Obad. 1), and goes on to describe how God would make Edom a small, despised nation (2), how God would bring down Edom in spite of its lofty and seemingly invincible

---

[7] Norman L. Geisler, *A Popular Survey of the Old Testament*, 252.

position in the mountains (3-4), how the judgment of God would leave behind less than thieves would leave after they have stolen and less than the grape-gatherers would leave in the field after the harvest (5), how the hidden treasures of Edom would be taken (6), how Edom would be the victim of a cruel plot (7), and how its wise men and strong men would be destroyed (8-9). The devastation brought on by God's judgment against Edom would be so severe that they would "be as though they had never been" (Obad. 16), and "no survivor" would be left to them (18).[8, 9]

4. Obadiah reflects the historical relationship between Edom and Israel. The prophet continually refers to Edom as "Esau" (Obad. 6, 8, 9, 18, 19, 21), and points out that Edom's treatment of Judah was particularly reprehensible due to the fact that Edom's behavior characterized the exact opposite of how one should treat his "brother" (10, 12). By referring to Edom as "Esau" (Obad. 6), the book presents a reminder that the Edomites were the descendants of Esau, the son of Isaac and brother of Jacob (Gen. 25:19-26, 32; 36:1-43), and as such, were related to the Israelites (Deut. 23:7). From the time that Israel departed from Egypt to travel to Canaan, Edom historically treated Israel in the general manner described by Obadiah (cf. Obad. 10; Num. 20:14-21). Although the book of Obadiah condemns Edom for not treating Judah as a "brother" should (Obad. 10, 12), this was actually the manner in which Edom had always behaved toward Israel in following the example set forth by Esau, the father of the nation (Gen. 27:41).[10]

Outline of Obadiah

I. The Coming Destruction of Edom (1-14).
    A. The certainty of God's judgment (1-9).
    B. The reasons for God's judgment (10-14).

II. The Coming Deliverance of Israel (15-21).
    A. The punishment of the nations (15-16).
    B. The deliverance of God's people (17-21).

Conclusion

The book of Obadiah presents God's case against Edom along with a description of His judgment against Edom and the surrounding nations. Obadiah emphasizes the manner in which God would punish Edom for mistreating Judah, while also looking forward to the future deliverance that would be made available to God's people through His kingdom.

---

[8] "As to the fulfillment of this doom upon Edom, it may be fairly inferred from Mal. 1:3-5 that by Malachi's time (ca. 435 B.C.) the Edomites had already been driven from Sela and Mount Seir by the overwhelming forces of the Nabatean Arabs" (Gleason L. Archer, *A Survey of Old Testament Introduction*, 337).

[9] The descendants of the Edomites disappeared from history after the destruction of Jerusalem by the Romans in A.D. 70 (Merrill C. Tenney, Ed., *The Zondervan Pictorial Bible Dictionary*, 234).

[10] The descendants of Esau were in constant conflict with the descendants of Jacob throughout the Old Testament (Num. 20:14-20; 1 Sam. 14:47; 1 Kings 11:14-25; 2 Chron. 20:1-22; 21:8; Psa. 137:7).

Notes

Questions

1. What is the meaning of the name "Obadiah," and how does the prophet's name provide a contrast to Edom? _____

_____

2. What information within the book would seem to indicate that Obadiah was a citizen of the southern kingdom of Judah (Obad. 11, 12, 17, 20-21)? _____

_____

3. What evidence within the book would seem to point to a time period prior to the Babylonian conquest of Judah for the events Obadiah describes?

   a. Obad. 11-14; 2 Chron. 21:8-10, 16-17. _____

_____

   b. Obad. 19. _____

   c. Obad. 1-9; Jer. 49:7-21. _____

   d. Obad. 17; Joel 2:32. _____

   e. Obad. 11. _____

   f. Obad. 20. _____

4. How does the message of Obadiah concerning Edom differ from his message concerning Judah (Obad. 15-16, 17-21)? _____

_____

5. How did God view Edom for standing by while Judah was plundered by enemies (Obad. 11)? _____

_____

6. How would Obadiah's prophecy concerning the kingdom ultimately be fulfilled (Obad. 21; Col. 1:13-14)? _____

_____

_____

7. According to Obadiah, what was the connection between the country of Edom and the deceitful pride of Edom (Obad. 3-9)? _____

_____

8. How had Edom sinned according to the following passages?

   a. Obad. 10. _____

   b. Obad. 11. _____

   c. Obad. 12. _____

d. Obad. 13. _____

e. Obad. 14. _____

9. According to the following passages, how does Obadiah describe the severity of God's judgment against Edom?

a. Obad. 1. _____

b. Obad. 2. _____

c. Obad. 3-4. _____

d. Obad. 5. _____

e. Obad. 6. _____

f. Obad. 7. _____

e. Obad. 8-9. _____

f. Obad. 16. _____

g. Obad. 18. _____

10. Why does Obadiah refer to Edom as "Esau," and what is the significance of this reference in light of the manner in which Edom had treated Israel (Obad. 6, 10)? _____

_____

Jonah

Introduction

Jonah is the thirty-second book of the Old Testament. The book of Jonah is generally recognized as the tenth of the seventeen Old Testament books of prophecy (Isaiah through Malachi), and is the fifth of the twelve books of the Minor Prophets (Hosea through Malachi). The theme of Jonah concerns the mercy and compassion of God, which would extend even to those Gentiles who repent (Jon. 3:6-10). The book of Jonah is unique among the books of the prophets in that, rather than containing a prophetic discourse, it contains a biographical account of certain events that took place in the life of the prophet resulting from his response to God's call to go and prophesy against Nineveh (Jon. 1:1-3). The story of Jonah is, perhaps, one of the most well-known stories of the Bible.

Origin of Jonah

1. *Title.* The book of Jonah is appropriately named for Jonah, the son of Amittai, the prophet of God, whose story forms the basis for the content of the book (Jon. 1:1-2). The prophet's name means "dove."[1]

2. *Author.* The opening statement of the book presents the claim that it contains a record of Jonah's response to the work which God commanded him to perform (Jon. 1:1-2). The prophet Jonah was a citizen of the northern kingdom of Israel from the town of Gath Hepher (2 Kings 14:25), which was located in the territory of the tribe of Zebulun (Josh. 19:13).[2] Jonah prophesied during the reign of Jeroboam II, king of Israel (2 Kings 14:23-25). Though he is mentioned in both the Old and New Testaments (2 Kings 14:25; Matt. 12:39-41; 16:4; Luke 11:29-32), little is known concerning the life and work of Jonah aside from what is recorded in the book that bears his name. However, it would appear that Jonah was a contemporary of the prophets Hosea and Amos.

3. *Date.* While the book itself does not provide a definite time period for the events it relates, the Bible does associate the prophet Jonah with Jeroboam the son of Joash, king of Israel (2 Kings 14:23-25). Since Jeroboam II reigned from 793-753 B.C., the story recorded in the book of Jonah must have taken place at some point during this period of time.[3] Therefore, it seems likely that the book would have been written sometime around 760 B.C.[4]

---

[1] Gleason L. Archer, *A Survey of Old Testament Introduction*, 341.

[2] The fact that Jonah was from a part of the country near Nazareth in Galilee serves to demonstrate the prideful ignorance of the Pharisees, who confidently dismissed the notion that a prophet could come from Galilee (John 7:45-52).

[3] Charles Dyer and Eugene Merrill, *Nelson's Old Testament Survey*, 771.

[4] Gleason L. Archer, *A Survey of Old Testament Introduction*, 342.

Purpose of Jonah

1. Historical purpose. The historical purpose of Jonah is to record the manner in which God used Jonah, an Israelite prophet, to persuade the inhabitants of the Assyrian city of Nineveh to repent when faced with the prospect of impending judgment (Jon. 1:1-2; 3:1-10). The book of Jonah demonstrates the fact that, even in ancient times, God was concerned for the spiritual wellbeing of people and nations other than Israel (Jon. 1:2; 4:11). Additionally, the book of Jonah would serve to contrast the stubborn and rebellious character of the Israelites, who refused to repent even though God constantly sent prophets among them, with the Ninevites, who repented almost immediately when confronted with the message of the prophet Jonah (Jon. 3:4-5).

2. Doctrinal purpose. Jonah is intended to teach that the mercy and grace of God are not restricted by national boundaries (Jon. 1:2, 14-16; 3:1-10) or by the selfishness and prejudices of men (4:1-3, 11; cf. Acts 10:34-35). The book also teaches that, while God's judgments against wickedness are severe (Jon. 3:4), His true desire is that all sinners should come to repentance (3:6-10; 4:1; cf. 2 Pet. 3:9; 1 Tim. 2:3-4). Additionally, the book of Jonah teaches that it is both foolish and futile for man to try to hide his actions and attitudes from God (Jon. 1:3-4; 4:1-11; cf. Heb. 4:13). Jonah emphasizes the fact that the mercy which God bestows on those who repent should be viewed as a cause for rejoicing, rather than be viewed from a selfish perspective (Jon. 4:1-4).

3. How does Jonah relate to Jesus Christ? Since Christ is the overall theme of the Bible, the book of Jonah relates to Him in some important ways. Although the book lacks any prophetic statement of Jonah regarding the coming of Christ, the three days which Jonah spent in the belly of the fish prophetically symbolized the three days which Christ would spend in the tomb prior to His resurrection (Jon. 1:17; 2:10; Matt. 12:40). Also, while the people of Nineveh repented upon hearing the preaching of Jonah (Jon. 3:1-5), the Jews of Jesus' day refused to repent even upon hearing the preaching of one infinitely greater than the prophet Jonah (Matt. 12:41; Luke 11:32).

Content of Jonah

1. Jonah contains a story in the life of the prophet Jonah. Unlike the other books of the prophets which consist largely of the messages God sent the prophets to proclaim, the book of Jonah scarcely mentions the prophet's message (Jon. 3:4), and instead focuses on a series of events which took place in his life. The story opens by relating God's command for Jonah to travel to Nineveh in order to pronounce divine judgment upon the city because of its great wickedness (Jon. 1:1-2). Rather than obey the command of God, Jonah boards a ship going to Tarshish in an effort to flee from His presence (Jon. 1:3).[5] While Jonah is aboard the ship God causes a storm to beat violently against it to the point where the situation appears hopeless (Jon. 1:1-4-5). Once the sailors discover Jonah sleeping in the ship and learn that he is fleeing from God, they become even more afraid and come to recognize the terrible storm as a direct conse-

---

[5] Tarshish should most likely be identified with a city in southwest Spain (Charles Dyer and Eugene Merrill, *Nelson's Old Testament Survey*, 774).

Notes

quence of Jonah's disobedience (Jon. 1:5-10). At Jonah's insistence, the men throw him overboard, the sea becomes calm (Jon. 1:11-15), and the sailors offer a sacrifice and make vows to the God of heaven (1:16). Meanwhile, God has prepared a "great fish," which swallows Jonah as he is descending into the depths of the sea (Jon. 1:17).[6] While in the belly of the fish, Jonah prays a prayer of thanksgiving to God, who has saved him from drowning to death, and expresses his intention to be obedient from this point forward (Jon. 3:1-9). After three days the fish vomits Jonah onto dry land (Jon. 1:17; 2:10), and when he is called by God a second time to go preach to Nineveh, the prophet responds obediently by traveling to the city and presenting a message of divine judgment (3:1-4). Once the people of Nineveh hear the preaching of Jonah, they believe the message and repent in sackcloth and ashes (Jon. 3:5-6). The king himself issues a proclamation commanding his subjects to fast and cry out to God for mercy (3:7-9). God then mercifully responds to the repentance of the Ninevites by sparing them from destruction (Jon. 3:10), but God's mercy toward them only angers Jonah, who would have rather seen Nineveh destroyed (4:1-4). As Jonah sits outside the city, God demonstrates the irrationality of Jonah's thinking by pointing out that the prophet cares more about a damaged and withered plant than he does about the people of Nineveh, including those who are innocent of any wrongdoing (Jon. 4:5-11). The story is brought to a close with God's admonition of the prophet.

2. Jonah involves a story that has been variously interpreted. Due to the story it presents, the book of Jonah has been subjected to various interpretations and has been attacked by critics of the Bible perhaps as much or more than any other book.[7] The mythical interpretation holds that the story of Jonah being swallowed alive by a great fish, or whale (Jon. 1:17-2:10), is too fanciful to be taken seriously and, therefore, the story should be treated as an ancient work of fiction containing elements that are borrowed from other sources and cultures. The allegorical interpretation views the book of Jonah as a figurative story which is meant to convey a deeper meaning, in which Jonah represents disobedient Israel (Jon. 1:3), the sea represents the Gentiles (1:12), and the three days spent in the belly of the fish represents the period of the Babylonian captivity (1:17).[8] The historical interpretation holds that the story of Jonah is the record of actual events that took place in the life of the prophet as he was literally called by God to preach to the city of Nineveh (Jon. 1:1-2; 3:1-2). Of these three interpretations, the historical view is the only one that

---

[6] "Incidentally, it should be observed that the Hebrew text of Jonah 2:1 actually reads *dag gadol*, or "great fish," rather than a technical term for "whale." But since Hebrew possessed no special word for "whale," and since no true fish—as opposed to marine mammal—is known to possess a stomach as capacious as a whale's, it is reasonable to adhere to the traditional interpretation at this point" (Gleason L. Archer, *A Survey of Old Testament Introduction*, 342).

[7] H. I. Hester, *The Heart of Hebrew History*, 279-280.

[8] "A closer examination of the text, however, shows that numerous features of the narrative can scarcely be fitted into the allegorical pattern. If the whale represented Babylon, what did Nineveh represent? As for the ship that set sail from Joppa, it is hard to see what this would correspond to in the allegory; nor is it clear why three days should be selected to represent seventy years of captivity" (Gleason L. Archer, *A Survey of Old Testament Introduction*, 343).

can be consistently applied and is the only one that is legitimate, since: (a) Jonah was a real historical figure (cf. 2 Kings 14:25; Jon. 1:1); (b) the book presents the story as a straightforward historical narrative; and (c) Jesus Christ referred to the events described in the book of Jonah as real historical events, including the preservation of Jonah in the belly of the fish (cf. Jon. 1:17; Matt. 12:40) and the impact of Jonah's preaching on the people of Nineveh (cf. Jon. 3:3-9; Matt. 12:41).[9]

3. Jonah presents a story that would become a sign. One of the most profound purposes of the story of Jonah is to serve as an illustration of what would be accomplished by Jesus Christ (Matt. 16:1-4). The story of Jonah spending three days and nights in the belly of the fish (Jon. 1:17) and being vomited out of the fish alive (2:10), would serve as a sign prefiguring the actual death, three-day entombment, and resurrection of Jesus (Matt. 12:38-40). Additionally, the record of Jonah bringing the Gentile inhabitants of Nineveh to repentance through the preaching of God's word (Jon. 3:1-9) would serve as a sign to those Jews who would reject the preaching of Jesus, even though they were God's covenant people and even though He was far greater than the prophet Jonah (Matt. 12:41; Luke 11:32). In this manner, the story presented in the book of Jonah becomes an exceptionally important story in relation to the story of Jesus Christ.

4. Jonah deals with attitudes. The book opens with the command of God for Jonah to proclaim divine judgment against Nineveh (Jon. 1:1-2), followed by Jonah's attempt to flee from God and from his responsibilities (1:3). Later, the prophet admits that his reason for fleeing was due to his unwillingness for the Ninevites to be granted the opportunity to repent and avoid destruction, which opportunity his preaching would surely afford (Jon. 3:10-4:1-2). Though Jonah preached to the people of Nineveh, his attitude was such that he hoped to see their doom, rather than their deliverance (Jon. 4:1-5). In fact, Jonah's attitude toward Nineveh was so poor that he became angry to the point of wishing for his own death upon realizing that Nineveh would not be punished in the manner that he had hoped (Jon. 4:3). It should be noted that, while Jonah was sent to preach to the Gentiles (Jon. 3:2), his story was recorded for God's covenant people who needed to learn that an attitude such as that displayed by Jonah is unacceptable to God. On the other hand, God's attitude throughout the book is one of mercy and longsuffering, as seen in His willingness to spare the life of His rebellious and ill-tempered prophet (Jon. 1:17-2:10) and in His willingness to relent from destroying the penitent Ninevites (3:10). A final attempt is made by God at the close of the book to mould Jonah's attitude so that it will conform to His own (Jon. 4:6-11).

Outline of Jonah

I. Jonah's Disobedience (1:1-17).
   A. The command of God for Jonah to preach to Nineveh (1:1-2).
   B. The rebellious response of Jonah (1:3)

---

[9] Jonah's reference to the king as "king of Nineveh" (Jon. 3:6), rather than as "king of Assyria," has also been used by critics to disprove the historicity of the story. However, the Old Testament sometimes refers to kings of various nations as being kings of the capital cities of their respective realms (cf. 1 Kings 21:1; 2 Chron. 24:23), so this sort of reference is not unique to Jonah.

Notes

Notes

C. The chastening of God upon Jonah (1:4-16).

D. The deliverance of Jonah through the fish prepared by God (1:17).

II. Jonah's Prayer (2:1-10).

    A. The prayer of Jonah from the belly of the fish (2:1-9).

    B. The release of Jonah from the belly of the fish (2:10).

III. Jonah's Preaching (3:1-10).

    A. The second command of God for Jonah to preach the Nineveh (3:1-2).

    B. The message of Jonah to the Ninevites (3:3-4).

    C. The repentance of the Ninevites (3:5-9).

    D. The mercy of God toward the Ninevites (3:10).

IV. Jonah's Anger (4:1-11).

    A. The complaint of Jonah concerning God's mercy (4:1-3).

    B. The lesson presented by God concerning His mercy (4:4-11).

Conclusion

The book of Jonah presents a unique story concerning God's desire for a Gentile nation to be brought to repentance so that He might show His mercy in them. Jonah emphasizes the futility of fighting against God and the necessity of adopting the merciful attitude of God, while providing a profound illustration of the death, burial, and resurrection of Christ.

Questions

1. How is the book of Jonah different from the other Minor Prophets?

_____

_____

2. What is known of Jonah's background, and with which king of Israel is his career as a prophet associated (Jon. 1:1; 2 Kings 14:25)? _____

_____

3. What may be learned from the fact that God sent Jonah to preach to a Gentile city such as Nineveh (Jon. 1:1-2; 4:11)? _____

_____

4. According to the book of Jonah, how should God's people respond when His mercy is shown to those who repent of their sins (Jon. 4:1-4, 11)? _____

_____

5. What connection is there between the preaching of Jonah in Nineveh, and the preaching of Jesus in Israel (Jon. 3:1-5; Matt. 12:41)? _____

_____

6. How does the portion of the story dealing with the plant demonstrate Jonah's irrational approach to God's merciful treatment of Nineveh (Jon. 4:5-11)? _____

_____

_____

7. What purposes were served by God causing a fish to swallow Jonah (Jon. 1:17-2:10)? _____

_____

8. Describe the following three approaches that have been used to interpret the book of Jonah and explain why the story should be viewed as historical.

a. Mythical. _____

b. Allegorical. _____

c. Historical. _____

9. How would the story of Jonah serve as a sign to those of Jesus' day (Jon. 1:17; Matt. 12:38-40)? _____

_____

_____

10. Why did Jonah attempt to flee to Tarshish rather than preach to Nineveh, and what does this demonstrate concerning his attitude (Jon. 1:1-3; 4:1-2)? _____

_____

_____

Notes

Micah

Introduction

Micah is the thirty-third book of the Old Testament. The book of Micah is generally recognized as the eleventh of the seventeen Old Testament books of prophecy (Isaiah through Malachi), and is the sixth of the twelve books of the Minor Prophets (Hosea through Malachi). The theme of Micah concerns the need for justice and holiness in the lives of the people of God (Mic. 6:8), and emphasizes the fact that they would be punished for lacking these characteristics by a God who is perfectly just and holy (3:9-12). The book of Micah pronounces doom upon both Israel (Mic. 1:6) and Judah (4:10) for their sins, while at the same time offering hope of salvation for the faithful (4:6-8; 7:18-20). The message of Micah is one that seeks to defend the poor against the oppression of the rich (Mic. 2:1-2; 3:1-3; 6:11-12).

Origin of Micah

1. Title. The book of Micah is appropriately named for Micah of Moresheth, the prophet of God, whose prophecies make up the content of the book (Mic. 1:1). The name Micah means, "Who is like Jehovah?"[1] The prophet's name is significant in that it reflects his message (Mic. 7:18).

2. Author. The opening statement of the book presents the claim that it contains the words that God directed Micah to speak concerning Israel and Judah (Mic. 1:1). The prophet Micah was a citizen of the southern kingdom of Judah from the town of Moresheth (Mic. 1:1), which was located about twenty miles southwest of Jerusalem.[2] Micah prophesied in Judah during the reigns of the kings Jotham, Ahaz, and Hezekiah (Mic. 1:1). Though almost nothing is known of Micah outside of the book that bears his name, it is important to note that his work was still well-known to the inhabitants of Judah a century later in the time of the prophet Jeremiah (Jer. 26:16-19; cf. Mic. 3:12). Micah prophesied in Judah during the same period of time as the prophet Isaiah (cf. Mic. 1:1; Isa. 1:1).

3. Date. Since Micah prophesied during the reigns of Jotham, Ahaz, and Hezekiah (Mic. 1:1), his work must have taken place between 739 and 686 B.C.[3] It is evident that Micah must have begun prophesying before the Assyrian conquest of the northern kingdom of Israel, which took place in 722 B.C., since he begins his message by warning of the fall of Samaria, the capital city of the northern kingdom (Mic. 1:6-7).[4] The time-frame for Micah's work may be narrowed down further since he proph-

[1] Gleason L. Archer, *A Survey of Old Testament Introduction*, 359.

[2] *Ibid.*, 360.

[3] Charles Dyer and Eugene Merrill, *Nelson's Old Testament Survey*, 779-780.

[4] *Ibid.*, 780.

esies of Judah's deliverance from the Assyrian invasion during the reign of Hezekiah, which took place in 701 B.C. (Mic. 5:5-6; cf. 2 Kings 18-19).[5] Therefore, a good estimate for the time period of Micah's prophetic career is from about 735 to 700 B.C., with the book having been completed sometime around the close of this period.[6]

Purpose of Micah

1. Historical purpose. The historical purpose of Micah is to record the manner in which God set forth His complaint against His people, who had openly transgressed His covenant (Mic. 1:2; 6:1-2). The book of Micah describes the various ways in which God's people had sinned against Him, both in their unjust treatment of one another (Mic. 2:1-2; 3:1-3, 8-11; 6:9-16), and in their unholy approach to their God (2:6-11; 3:4-7). Additionally, Micah warned Israel and Judah of the coming judgment of God which would result in the destruction of both kingdoms (Mic. 1:3-5, 6-7; 2:3-4; 3:12; 4:10; 6:13), while at the same time offering hope of restoration and salvation for the faithful remnant (2:12-13; 4:1-8; 5:2-5; 7:16-20).

2. Doctrinal purpose. Micah is intended to teach that, while God hates sin and stands ready to punish those who do evil (Mic. 1:3-5), He also stands ready to pardon the iniquities of those who truly repent and turn to Him (7:18-20). The book also teaches that, while man tends to make it very complicated to serve God (Mic. 6:6-7), what God actually desires of man is really very simple (6:8). Additionally, the book of Micah teaches that God's infinite power and compassionate character are incomparable (Mic. 2:7; 7:18). Micah emphasizes the necessity of justice in man's dealings with his fellow man (Mic. 3:1), and holiness in man's approach to God (3:4).

3. How does Micah relate to Jesus Christ? Since Christ is the overall theme of the Bible, the book of Micah relates to Him in some important ways. Micah portrays Christ as the king who will shepherd His people (Mic. 2:12-13) establish the Lord's house (4:1-3), reign over His kingdom (4:6-8), and bring about the forgiveness and salvation of His people (7:7-20). Micah contains one of the most striking messianic prophecies of the Old Testament in which the prophet presents Christ as the king who will be born in Bethlehem, though He has existed from eternity (Mic. 5:2-5; cf. Matt. 2:1-2).[7]

Content of Micah

1. Micah emphasizes the sins and punishments of God's covenant people. As the prophet states, one of the primary reasons for his message is to expose the manner in which Israel and Judah transgressed God's covenant (Mic. 3:8). Micah addresses the numerous sins of Israel and Judah, including idolatry (Mic. 1:7; 5:13-14), covetousness (2:1-2),

---

[5] *Ibid.*

[6] Norman L. Geisler, *A Popular Survey of the Old Testament*, 248.

[7] "In verse 2 the future birth of the Messianic King is declared. His humanity is set forth in that He is to come forth out of Bethlehem, and His true deity, in that the places of His going forth (*motsa'othau*) are from of yore (*miqqedem*), from days of eternity (*mime'olam*)" (Edward J. Young, *An Introduction to the Old Testament*, 269).

The Taylor Prism contains the Assyrian record of Sennacherib's invasion of Judah during the reign of King Hezekiah. He conquered many of Judah's cities and shut up Hezekiah in Jerusalem "like a bird in a cage."

false prophecy (2:6-11; 3:6-7, 11), oppression of the poor (2:8-9; 3:1-3), corrupt worship (3:4; 6:6-8), injustice and corruption on the part of the leaders (3:9-11; 7:3), sorcery (5:12), dishonest business practices (6:10-11), violence and deception (6:12; 7:2-4), a willingness to follow the statutes of wicked kings rather than the law of God (6:16), and dishonorable treatment of family members (7:5-6).[8] As a direct consequence of these sins, God's judgment would fall severely upon His people (Mic. 2:3-4) in the form of the Assyrian conquest and deportation of Israel (1:6-7), and the Babylonian conquest of captivity Judah (3:12; 4:10-13). The situation with respect to sin was so dismal in the days of Micah that the prophet laments the incredible scarcity of faithful and upright men (Mic. 7:2).

2. Micah presents God's case against His people. In rebuking Israel and Judah for their sins, Micah employs the imagery of a lawsuit in which God takes His people to court for violating His covenant with them and forcefully establishes His case against them (Mic. 1:2). God places His people on trial, commanding them to plead their "case" (Mic. 6:1), as He sets forth His "complaint" and brings charges against them (6:2). As the trial proceeds, God asks His people to bring forth any evidence they might use in order to testify against Him (Mic. 6:3). While it is obvious that the people have no evidence to present against God, He goes on to present specific evidence for His faithfulness, including the fact that He redeemed them from the bondage of Egypt (Mic. 6:4), prevented Balaam from cursing them in the wilderness, and brought them safely into the Promised Land (6:5). In response to the charges brought by God and the lack of evidence with which to provide a defense, the people (in the voice of one man) suppose that the solution to the problem is to offer more sacrifices, perhaps even a human sacrifice, in order to turn away God's wrath (Mic. 6:6-7). However, God responds by pointing out that the only acceptable solution is for His people to start living according to the precepts of the covenant (6:8; cf. Deut. 10:12-13). Speaking on behalf of his people, the prophet acknowledges that he stands guilty as charged and is left with no other option than to face the just judgment of God (Mic. 7:9), while looking forward to eventual redemption and restoration (7:10-20).

3. Micah contains three cycles. Following its introduction (Mic. 1:1), the book may be viewed as consisting of three successive cycles, each addressing sin and judgment followed by prophecies of salvation and hope for the future. The first cycle (Mic. 1:2-2:13) opens with the prophet addressing the sins of Israel and Judah, both generically (1:5) and specifically (2:1-2, 6-11), pronouncing judgment on the people for their sins (1:6-7, 8-16; 2:3-5), and then moving on to a message of hope consisting in the future restoration of a faithful remnant which would be shepherded by the Lord (2:12-13). The second cycle (Mic. 3:1-5:15) returns to the

---

[8] The significance of God's charge concerning the willingness of His people to follow after the ways of Omri and Ahab, lies in the fact that these men were two of the most wicked kings of Israel (Mic. 6:16; cf. 1 Kings 16:25, 33; 21:25).

prophet addressing the sins of God's people (3:1-3, 8-11), pronouncing judgment on them for these sins (3:4-7, 12), and then providing hope for the future by describing the establishment of the Lord's house (4:1-5), the salvation of a faithful remnant in the Lord's kingdom (4:6-8), the coming of the everlasting king (5:2-5), and the defeat of the wicked (5:6-15). The third cycle (Mic. 6:1-7:20) returns once more to a discussion of the sins of God's people (6:1-12, 16; 7:1-6), and a discussion of the judgment that would result from these sins (6:13-16), followed by a message of salvation and redemption centered on the hope of obtaining forgiveness through God's mercy (7:7-20).

4. Micah includes a message similar to that of Isaiah. In light of the fact that Micah and Isaiah were both called by God to prophesy to the same people during the same period of time (cf. Mic. 1:1; Isa. 1:1), it should not be surprising to find that they often present essentially the same message. The most obvious example of similarity between the content of Micah and Isaiah is found in the prophecy of the establishment of the Lord's house (cf. Mic. 4:1-3; Isa. 2:1-4), in which the message of the two prophets is virtually identical.[9] Other points of similarity between the messages of Micah and Isaiah include: (a) prophecies of Judah being taken captive to Babylon (cf. Mic. 4:10; Isa. 39:6); (b) prophecies of the birth of the Savior and king (cf. Mic. 5:2-3; Isa. 9:6-7); (c) prophecies concerning God's deliverance of Judah from the Assyrian threat (cf. Mic. 5:5-6; Isa. 14:24-25); and (d) prophecies of the restoration of the remnant of God's people from foreign lands (cf. Mic. 7:12; Isa. 11:11).

Outline of Micah

I. God's Judgment Against His People (1:1-2:13).
   A. Condemnation of the sins of the people (1:1-2:11).
   B. First promise of restoration through the Messiah (2:12-13).

II. God's Wrath Against His People (3:1-5:15).
   A. Condemnation of the leaders of the people (3:1-12).
   B. Second promise of restoration through the Messiah (4:1-5:15).

III. God's Case Against His People (6:1-7:20).
   A. Condemnation of the injustice of the people (6:1-7:6).
   B. Third promise of restoration through the Messiah (7:7-20).

Conclusion

The book of Micah presents God's case against His people along with the punishment they would be forced to endure for transgressing His covenant. However, Micah also emphasizes the hope of salvation to which the faithful remnant could cling by looking forward to the coming of the Christ, whom Micah depicts as the everlasting king and shepherd of God's people who would dispense His mercy and compassion.

---

[9] The prophecy of the establishment of the Lord's house finds its fulfillment in the church, which was established in the latter days (cf. Mic. 4:1; Acts 2:14-21; 41-47), is considered the house of God (cf. Mic. 4:2; 1 Tim. 3:15; Eph. 2:19-22), began at Jerusalem (cf. Mic. 4:2; Acts 1:8), and is made up of people of all nations (cf. Mic. 4:1-2; Eph. 2:14-16).

Notes

Questions

1. What is the meaning of Micah's name, and how is the meaning of the prophet's name connected to the content of his message (Mic. 7:18)?

_____

_____

2. What is known of Micah's background, and how much of an impact did his message have (Mic. 1:1; 3:12; Jer. 26:16-19)? _____

_____

3. How were God's people treating one another during Micah's day?

a. Mic. 2:1-2. _____

b. Mic. 3:1-3. _____

c. Mic. 3:8-11. _____

d. Mic. 6:9-16. _____

4. According to Micah, what is so impressive about God's attitude toward sin (Mic. 1:3-5; 7:18-20)? _____

_____

5. What important truths concerning Christ are presented in Micah's prophecy of the coming ruler (Mic. 5:2-5)? _____

_____

6. Describe the sins of God's people which are discussed in the following passages.

a. Mic. 1:7. _____

b. Mic. 2:1-2. _____

c. Mic. 2:8-9. _____

d. Mic. 3:10-11. _____

e. Mic. 6:10-11. _____

f. Mic. 6:16. _____

g. Mic. 7:5-6. _____

7. What language does Micah employ to indicate that God is bringing a lawsuit against His people?

a. Mic. 1:2. _____

b. Mic. 6:1. _____

c. Mic. 6:2. _____

d. Mic. 6:3. _____

8. What evidence does God provide in order to demonstrate His loyalty to Israel (Mic. 6:3-5)? _____

_____

9. How did God's people intend to solve the problem of the guilt of their sins, and why was their solution unacceptable (Mic. 6:6-8)? _____

_____

10. Why do the books of Micah and Isaiah contain many similar prophecies (Mic. 4:1-3; Isa. 2:1-4)? _____

_____

Nahum

Notes

Introduction

Nahum is the thirty-fourth book of the Old Testament. The book of Nahum is generally recognized as the twelfth of the seventeen Old Testament books of prophecy (Isaiah through Malachi), and is the seventh of the twelve books of the Minor Prophets (Hosea through Malachi). The theme of Nahum concerns the absolute holiness and righteousness of God, leading both to judgment against His enemies (Nah. 1:2), as well as to the protection of those who trust in Him (1:7). The book of Nahum pronounces doom upon Nineveh, the mighty capital city of Assyria (Nah. 1:1; 2:8-10), which had been responsible for cruelly oppressing the people of God (1:15). While the preaching of the prophet Jonah had brought the Ninevites temporarily to repentance more than a century earlier (Jon. 3:1-10), the message of Nahum is that the time for Nineveh to be punished has arrived and the judgment will not be altered (Nah. 3:18-19).

Origin of Nahum

1. Title. The book of Nahum is appropriately named for Nahum the Elkoshite, the prophet of God, whose prophecies make up the content of the book (Nah. 1:1). The prophet's name means "comfort" or "consolation," which is significant in light of the fact that Judah would be comforted through the downfall of Nineveh (Nah. 1:12-13, 15), while Nineveh would have no one to comfort her (3:7, 19).[1]

2. Author. The opening statement of the book presents the claim that it contains the record of the vision which God delivered to Nahum the Elkoshite concerning the destruction of Nineveh (Nah. 1:1). The location of Elkosh, the city with which the prophet is identified (Nah. 1:1), has yet to be resolved, though various locations have been put forward, including: (a) the town of Elkesi in Galilee; (b) the city of Capernaum, whose name means, "village of Nahum" and has traditionally been associated with the prophet; (c) the city of Alqush near Mosul in Assyria; and (d) the village of Elcesei, which was located midway between Jerusalem and Gaza.[2] While the exact location of the city of the prophet's origin remains unknown, the evidence seems to suggest that Nahum was a citizen of Judah, since that is where his concern lies (Nah. 1:15). Nothing is known of Nahum outside of the book that bears his name.

3. Date. Though its lack of any exact historical marker makes is impossible to attach an exact date to the book of Nahum, certain events mentioned within the book provide a general time-frame. Since Nahum makes mention of the fall of the Egyptian city of No Amon (Thebes) as a well-known past event (Nah. 3:8-11), the prophecy of Nahum must be dated

---

[1] Charles Dyer and Eugene Merrill, *Nelson's Old Testament Survey*, 795.

[2] Gleason L. Archer, *A Survey of Old Testament Introduction*, 391.

sometime after the city fell to the Assyrian army in 661 B.C.[3] On the other hand, since Nahum foretells the fall of Nineveh (2:8-10), which took place in 612 B.C., the book must have been written prior to that time.[4] Since Nahum portrays Ninevah and the Assyrian Empire at the height of its power (Nah. 1:12; 3:12, 16), a good estimate for the date of his prophecy is sometime between the years 650 and 640 B.C.[5, 6]

Purpose of Nahum

1. Historical purpose. The historical purpose of Nahum is to record the manner in which God would execute His judgment upon Nineveh (Nah. 1:1; 2:8-10), and to describe how that proud and cruel city (3:1), which had been responsible for causing so many to suffer (1:12, 15; 2:11-12; 3:19), would be repaid for her sins (2:13; 3:4-7). The book of Nahum describes how the holiness and righteousness of the true God of heaven would be vindicated before the idolatrous Gentile nations through His judgment on Nineveh (Nah. 1:2-3, 7-11, 14; 3:5-7). Additionally, Nahum would serve to comfort Judah, which was struggling under the yoke of Assyrian dominance (Nah. 1:12-13), by announcing the coming destruction of Nineveh (1:15; 2:2).

2. Doctrinal purpose. Nahum is intended to teach that God is both just in His judgments against evil (Nah. 1:2-3), and good in His dealings with the righteous (1:7). The book also teaches that, while Israel was chosen to be God's covenant people through whom He would carry out His plan of redemption (Nah. 2:2), the Gentile nations were responsible for acknowledging and honoring the true God of heaven as well (1:2, 14; 3:4-5). Additionally, the book of Nahum teaches that even the most powerful nations, armies, and weapons of war are absolutely powerless when confronted with the wrath and judgment of Almighty God (Nah. 1:6, 12; 2:13; 3:8-13).

3. How does Nahum relate to Jesus Christ? Since Christ is the overall theme of the Bible, the book of Nahum relates to Him, as does every other book of the Old Testament. Nahum prophesies of one "who brings good tidings, who proclaims peace" (Nah. 1:15), thereby echoing the prophecy of Isaiah (cf. Isa. 52:7; Rom. 10:15), which would ultimately be fulfilled in the reign of Christ, who would bring lasting salvation and peace to His people.

Content of Nahum

1. Nahum praises the majesty of God. In order to establish that his prophecy against Nineveh will, in fact, be accomplished, Nahum begins his book by praising and magnifying the true God of heaven, whose judgment will result in Nineveh's fall (Nah. 1:1-2). Nahum praises God for His greatness by emphasizing His great power (Nah. 1:3), His control over storms and whirlwinds and His lofty position above the clouds (1:3), His

[3] Norman L. Geisler, *A Popular Survey of the Old Testament*, 255.

[4] Gleason L. Archer, *A Survey of Old Testament Introduction*, 392.

[5] Charles Dyer and Eugene Merrill, *Nelson's Old Testament Survey*, 796.

[6] These dates would place Nahum in the time period of the reigns of Mannasseh, Amon, and Josiah, kings of Judah (Norman L. Geisler, *A Popular Survey of the Old Testament*, 255).

ability to rebuke the sea and dry up the rivers (1:4), and the trembling of the earth in His presence (1:5). By ascribing such glory to God, Nahum demonstrates that it is well within His power to judge the wicked (Nah. 1:3), that the wicked will not be able to stand in the face of His wrath (1:6), and that any plans the wicked may devise against Him will be brought to nothing (1:9-11). Based on the praise which Nahum offers, there can be no doubt that such a majestic and powerful God would have little trouble in bringing even a powerful city like Nineveh to a complete end (Nah. 1:7-8, 12, 14; 2:13; 3:12-13).

2. *Nahum contains a poetic description of the fall of Nineveh.* Nahum describes the fall of Nineveh in great detail and makes clear the fact that the destruction of the city would come as a direct result of God's judgment (Nah. 2:13). The events leading up to Nineveh's destruction are summarized through a scene depicting the approach of an invading force as the Ninevites prepare to defend their city (Nah. 2:1, 3) by racing through the streets in chariots and manning their defensive positions (2:4-5). However, Nahum describes the great battle as one which would essentially be over as soon as it begins (Nah. 2:6), and one which would be followed by the inhabitants of Nineveh being taken captive (2:7), its army being scattered (2:8), its wealth being plundered (2:9), and the city itself being turned into a desolate wasteland (2:10).[7] Though Nineveh must have seemed invincible and impregnable (Nah. 1:12), it would be unable to defend itself against God's judgment any more than No Amon was able to defend itself against the Assyrian onslaught (2:8-11). Nineveh is depicted as stubble that would be easily burned (Nah. 1:10), its strongholds are depicted as ripe figs that are ready to be eaten (3:12), its inhabitants are depicted as defenseless women (3:13), the city is depicted as a field consumed by locusts (3:15-16), and its commanders are depicted as insects which flee away as soon as they feel the heat of the sun (3:17). As the one who would personally bring judgment upon Ninevah (Nah. 2:13; 3:5), God speaks directly to the city, saying, "I will dig your grave" (1:14), "I will burn your chariots" (2:13), "I will show the nations your nakedness" (3:5), and "I will cast abominable filth upon you" (3:6). In destroying the city, God would inflict upon Nineveh a wound which would never heal (Nah. 3:19).[8]

3. *Nahum provides the reasons for the fall of Nineveh.* While the intensity of God's judgment against Nineveh is described by Nahum as being especially severe (Nah. 3:19), the prophet explains that such a harsh judgment was made necessary by the intensity of Nineveh's sin and rebellion against God (1:11, 14). The sins of Nineveh are described by Nahum as including her unusually cruel and ruthless treatment of

---

[7] "Nahum 2:6 contains a remarkably exact prediction, for subsequent history records that a vital part of the city walls of Nineveh was carried away by a great flood, and this ruin of the defensive system permitted the besieging Medes and Chaldeans to storm the city without difficulty" (Gleason L. Archer, *A Survey of Old Testament Introduction*, 392).

[8] "Nineveh was destroyed by the combined armies of the Babylonians, Medes, and Scythians in 612 B.C. The city was destroyed so completely that the site was not even positively identified as Nineveh until the excavations of Botta and Layard in the mid 1800s" (Charles Dyer and Eugene Merrill, *Nelson's Old Testament Survey*, 796).

other nations (Nah. 3:1-3, 8-11), her willingness to prostitute herself for personal gain (3:4), and her extensive idolatry in place of worship of the true God (1:14). In keeping with the picture of Nineveh as an abominable harlot, Nahum describes her punishment in terms of God lifting her skirt in order to show her shame and nakedness to the nations which have been seduced by her wealth and prestige (Nah. 3:5), and casting "abominable filth" upon her (3:6), making her a horrible spectacle with whom none would dare associate themselves (3:6-7). Ultimately, the reason for God's judgment against Nineveh was due to the fact that she had made herself an enemy of God (Nah. 1:2-3).

4. Nahum reveals the character of God. In prophesying against Nineveh, Nahum emphasizes some key aspects of God's character which would demand that He punish the wicked city. Because God is a jealous God (Nah. 1:2), Nineveh must come under judgment for rejecting Him in favor of the worship of false gods (1:14). Because God is just (Nah. 1:3), it would be impossible for Nineveh to escape judgment due to the wicked course she has chosen to pursue. Because God is all-powerful (Nah. 1:3-6), there would be nothing that could stand in the way of Him properly executing His judgment upon Nineveh. Because God is good (Nah. 1:7-8), He must oppose Nineveh for having oppressed and abused the righteous.

Outline of Nahum

I. The Announcement of God's Judgment Against Nineveh (1:1-15).
    A. Introduction (1:1).
    B. God's character demands judgment against Nineveh (1:2-8).
    C. God's judgment against Nineveh will be final (1:9-15).

II. The Description of God's Judgment Against Nineveh (2:1-13).
    A. Nineveh's preparation for battle (2:1-4).
    B. Nineveh's defeat in battle (2:5-13).

III. The Explanation of God's Judgment Against Nineveh (3:1-19).
    A. Nineveh will have her sins exposed (3:1-7).
    B. Nineveh will fare no better than No Amon (3:8-11).
    C. Nineveh will be unable to resist the judgment of God (3:12-17).
    D. Nineveh will have no comfort (3:18-19).

Conclusion

The book of Nahum announces the terrible judgment which God would visit upon Nineveh as punishment for her sins. Nahum emphasizes the glory and majesty of God, whose perfect justice demands that He punish the wicked, while His perfect goodness demands that He avenge the righteous.

Notes

Questions

1. What is the meaning of Nahum's name, and how is the meaning of the prophet's name connected to the content of his message? _____

   _____

2. How do the events discussed in the following passages provide a definite time-frame during which the prophecy of Nahum must have been delivered?

   a. Nah. 3:8-11. _____

   b. Nah. 2:8-10. _____

3. Why would Nahum's message concerning the destruction of Nineveh serve as a comfort to Judah?

   a. Nah. 1:12-13. _____

   b. Nah. 1:15. _____

   c. Nah. 2:2. _____

4. How does the message of Nahum teach that God is at the same time both thoroughly just and thoroughly good (Nah. 1:2-3, 7)? _____

   _____

5. What does God's judgment against Nineveh teach concerning the responsibility of the Gentile nations toward God in the Old Testament (Nah. 1:2, 14; 3:4-5)? _____

   _____

6. Why does Nahum spend the first portion of the book praising God for His majesty and power (Nah. 1:1-8)? _____

   _____

7. How do the following passages depict the defenselessness of Nineveh in the face of God's judgment?

   a. Nah. 1:10. _____

   b. Nah. 3:12. _____

   c. Nah. 3:13. _____

   d. Nah. 3:15-16. _____

   e. Nah. 3:17. _____

8. How does Nahum describe the battle in which Nineveh would fall, and how would the outcome indicate that it would be decided by God (Nah. 2:5-10)? _____

   _____

   _____

9. For what sins would God punish Nineveh according to the following passages?

a. Nah. 1:14. _____

b. Nah. 3:1-3, 8-11. _____

c. Nah. 3:4. _____

10. How would the characteristics of God described in the following passages make it necessary for God to punish Nineveh?

a. Nah. 1:2. _____

b. Nah. 1:3. _____

c. Nah. 1:3-6. _____

d. Nah. 1:7-8. _____

Notes

Habakkuk

Introduction

Habakkuk is the thirty-fifth book of the Old Testament. The book of Habakkuk is generally recognized as the thirteenth of the seventeen Old Testament books of prophecy (Isaiah through Malachi), and is the eighth of the twelve books of the Minor Prophets (Hosea through Malachi). The theme of Habakkuk concerns the perfect holiness of God (Hab. 2:20), which prevents Him from tolerating sin (1:12), demands that He punish sin, even among His own covenant people (1:2-10), and provides the basis upon which the faithful should place their trust in Him (2:4; 3:17-19). The book of Habakkuk addresses the problem of maintaining one's faith in God in the midst of difficulties which obscure the fulfillment of His righteous promises (Hab. 1:2, 13-14; 2:1-4). The style of Habakkuk is unique among the books of the Minor Prophets, in that instead of simply bringing God's message to the people, the prophet brings the concerns of the people to God in an effort to learn His will (Hab. 1:2-4, 12-17; 2:1).

Origin of Habakkuk

1. Title. The book of Habakkuk is appropriately named for Habakkuk, the prophet of God, whose prophecies make up the content of the book (Hab. 1:1). The prophet's name probably means "embrace," which would seem to signify his work of embracing and comforting the faithful through a message which encourages constant trust in God (Hab. 2:4; 3:17-19).[1]

2. Author. The opening statement of the book presents the claim that it contains the record of the vision which God delivered to Habakkuk (Hab. 1:1), while the latter portion of the book claims to be the work of Habakkuk as well (3:1). The postscript attached to the end of the book, which instructs the prophet's song to be used in worship (Hab. 3:19), may indicate that Habakkuk was a Levite who lived in Jerusalem (cf. Psa. 81:1; 84:1).[2] Though nothing is known of the prophet Habakkuk outside of the book that bears his name, the New Testament writers quote authoritatively from his work (Rom. 1:17; Gal. 3:11; Heb. 10:38; cf. Hab. 2:4). Habakkuk was apparently a contemporary of the prophet Jeremiah (cf. Jer. 1:1-3).

3. Date. Though its lack of any exact historical marker makes it impossible to attach an exact date to the book of Habakkuk, certain conditions described within the book provide a general time-frame. Since Habakkuk prophesies concerning the rise of the Chaldeans (Babylonians), and speaks of their conquest of Judah as a future event (Hab. 1:5-11), it is clear that the book must have been written prior to the Babylonian conquest of Judah which began to take place in 605 B.C.[3] On the other hand,

---

[1] Gleason L. Archer, *A Survey of Old Testament Introduction*, 395.

[2] Norman L. Geisler, *A Popular Survey of the Old Testament*, 259.

[3] Charles Dyer and Eugene Merrill, *Nelson's Old Testament Survey*, 803.

since Habakkuk describes a situation in Judah in which the rulers fail to administer justice and instead plunder and oppress the people (Hab. 1:2-4), such a description would appear to fit the time period immediately following the death of Josiah, who was Judah's last good king, in 609 B.C.[4] Therefore, it seems most likely that Habakkuk delivered his message sometime around 608 or 607 B.C. during the early part of the reign of King Jehoiakim (cf. 2 Chron. 36:5-8).[5]

Purpose of Habakkuk

1. Historical purpose. The historical purpose of Habakkuk is to record the manner in which God comforted the faithful in Judah during the days of Habakkuk by promising to execute His judgment upon their wicked rulers through the Babylonian conquest (Hab. 1:1-11), and by promising, in due course, to execute His judgment on the wicked Babylonians as well (1:12-2:20).[6] The book of Habakkuk describes the suffering of the righteous in the midst of injustice (Hab. 1:2-4, 12-17), and shows how God would correct injustice through His own just judgment against sin (1:5-11; 2:5-20). Additionally, Habakkuk would encourage the faithful to live by faith in God (Hab. 2:4; 3:16, 17-19) even in the face of trying circumstances in the present (1:2-4) and the uncertainty of the Babylonian conquest in the future (1:5-11). The book of Habakkuk also briefly reviews the history of God's faithfulness toward His covenant people (Hab. 3:1-15).

2. Doctrinal purpose. Habakkuk is intended to teach that God is both holy and just in His dealings with man (Hab. 1:12; 2:20), and reigns supreme over even the most powerful nations (1:5-11; 2:3, 13, 20). The book also teaches that, while man may be confused and may question God's response to wickedness (Hab. 1:2-4, 12-17), ultimately, the faithful must realize that God is, in fact, in control (2:20), and must learn to patiently trust Him in spite of life's circumstances (2:3-4; 3:17-19). Additionally, the book of Habakkuk teaches that, though evil may appear to triumph for a time (Hab. 1:2-4), the faithful will be rewarded with good, while the proud will be destroyed (2:4, 5-8).

3. How does Habakkuk relate to Jesus Christ? Since Christ is the overall theme of the Bible, the book of Habakkuk relates to Him in some important ways. In recording the truth that "the just shall live by his faith" (Hab. 2:4), Habakkuk points to the justification which would ultimately come through faith in Christ and obedience to His gospel (cf. Rom. 1:16-17; Gal. 3:11-14). Also, the prophecy of Habakkuk concerning a time when "the earth will be filled with the knowledge of the glory of the Lord" (Hab. 2:14) is one which would find its ultimate fulfillment in the spread of the gospel of Christ throughout the world (cf. Matt. 28:18-20; Mark 16:15-16; Acts 1:8; Col. 1:23). Additionally, Habakkuk makes mention of God's

---

[4] Gleason L. Archer, *A Survey of Old Testament Introduction*, 396.

[5] *Ibid.*

[6] "The rapacious Jewish nobles, allied with corrupt religious leaders, were shamelessly robbing and oppressing the common people in Judah. Therefore they were to be punished through the instrumentality of the Chaldeans. It is interesting to note that it was the upper classes that were first taken into captivity in the two preliminary deportations of 605 and 597. The majority of the lower classes was left in the land until the third deportation of 586" (*Ibid.*, 397).

"Anointed," or "Messiah," in connection with His salvation (Hab. 3:13), which foreshadows Jesus Christ, God's Anointed Savior of mankind (cf. Luke 4:16-21; Acts 10:36-38).

Content of Habakkuk

1. Habakkuk presents a dialogue between the prophet and God. One of the most striking features of the book is its recorded conversation between God and Habakkuk which carries the prophet Habakkuk from doubt (Hab. 1:2) and perplexity (1:3, 12-17) to confident trust (2:20; 3:2) and faithful resolve (3:17-19). Habakkuk begins with the prophet's complaint arising from the fact that he has continually cried out against the wickedness, violence, and injustice taking place in Judah, and yet it appears that God has taken no action to correct these wrongs (Hab. 1:2-4). God then responds to the prophet's complaint by offering the assurance that He will punish the wicked among His people and is, in fact, making preparation to do so by raising up Babylon to serve as the instrument of His punishment (Hab. 1:5-10), though Babylon will also presumptuously transgress against Him (1:11). God's response then raises another question in the mind of the prophet, who cannot understand how a perfectly holy and righteous God could allow a wicked nation like Babylon to serve as the instrument of His punishment against a nation more righteous than itself (Hab. 1:12-17), and so resolves to wait for reproof and response from the mouth of God (2:1). By way of response, God informs Habakkuk that He will carry out His judgment just as previously stated, and that the righteous are expected to trust in Him (Hab. 2:2-4). However, He will also, in due time, punish Babylon for its sins (2:5-20). With his questions answered and his doubts settled, the prophet then expresses his praise for God and his determination to trust Him fully (Hab. 3:1-19).

2. Habakkuk pronounces woes against Babylon. Though Babylon would be used by God to punish His own wicked people (Hab. 1:5-11), Habakkuk relates how God would also punish Babylon for its pride, greed, and insatiable desire to cruelly expand its empire (2:5), and pronounces various woes against Babylon detailing God's just judgment against that nation (2:6-20). The first woe pronounced against Babylon proclaims that the nation which increased by plundering that which belonged to others would one day be plundered by others as a consequence of its own violence and oppression (Hab. 2:6-8). The second woe pronounced against Babylon proclaims that the nation which consolidated its power by preying upon others would stand condemned for the self-destructive course it has pursued (Hab. 2:9-11). The third woe pronounced against Babylon proclaims that the nation which builds itself up by tearing others down through murder and bloodshed would find that its labors have all been in vain since all that it worked to build will be destroyed (Hab. 2:12-14). The fourth woe pronounced against Babylon proclaims that the nation which has spread immorality and corruption for its own selfish purposes would find itself brought to shame and covered with violence (Hab. 2:15-17). The fifth woe pronounced against Babylon proclaims that the nation which has trusted in worthless idols will be forced to submit to the authority of the true God of heaven (Hab. 2:18-20). Habakkuk vividly describes how Babylon would make the transition from being the nation to administer

God's punishment to being on the receiving end of his punishment.[7]

3. Habakkuk includes the prophet's prayer. The book closes with a prayer of Habakkuk (Hab. 3:1-19) which is presented in the form of a psalm, as indicated by the musical notations provided at both its beginning and end (3:1, 19).[8] In response to God's answers to his questions (Hab. 1-2), the prophet breaks forth in praise to God, calling upon Him to exercise His just judgment, while at the same time asking Him to remember to show mercy to the faithful (3:2). Habakkuk's prayer begins by reviewing the history of how God exercised His mighty power throughout Israel's history in order to defeat their enemies (Hab. 3:3-11, 14-15), and provide what He promised them (3:12-13). Knowing the power of God and His past willingness to exercise that power to punish the wicked, the prophet expresses his conviction that God will punish Judah in the exact manner which He has revealed (Hab. 3:16). In spite of the impending judgment facing Judah, Habakkuk closes his prayer by expressing his resolve to confidently trust in God and rejoice in God, who alone provides strength and salvation, even in the midst of dire circumstances (Hab. 3:17-19).

4. Habakkuk focuses on faith. The book covers a spiritual journey of faith in the life of the prophet Habakkuk. Habakkuk's faith is tested through his observation of injustice and God's apparent lack of concern (Hab. 1:2-4), as well as through the difficulty proposed by God's use of a wicked nation like Babylon to administer His punishment against Judah (1:12-17). However, Habakkuk's faith is refined as he patiently waits for the wisdom of God's response to his questions (Hab. 2:1), and is taught that God's judgments are sure (2:2-3), that the just will live by faith in God (2:4), and that God would, in fact, punish Babylon as well in His own time (2:5-20). Finally, Habbakuk's faith emerges triumphant as he expresses his unwavering trust in God (3:3-15), whose words cause him to tremble (3:2, 16) and plead for mercy (3:2), but whose faithfulness causes him to rejoice even in extremely difficult times (3:17-19).

Outline of Habakkuk

I. Habakkuk's Dialogue with God (1:1-2:4).
   A. How can God allow Judah's sin to continue (1:1-11)?
   B. How can God use a wicked nation to punish Judah (1:12-2:4)?

II. . Habakkuk's Prophecy Against Babylon (2:5-20).
   A. First woe against Babylon (2:5-8).
   B. Second woe against Babylon (2:9-11).
   C. Third woe against Babylon (2:12-14).
   D. Fourth woe against Babylon (2:15-17).
   E. Fifth woe against Babylon (2:18-20).

III. Habakkuk's Prayer of Praise (3:1-19).
   A. The prophet's petition for mercy from God (3:1-2).
   B. The prophet's review of the past works of God (3:3-15).
   C. The prophet's confidence in the salvation of God (3:16-19).

---

[7] Babylon fell to a coalition of the Medes and Persians in 539 B.C. having been conquered by the Persian king, Cyrus the Great (*Ibid.*, 366).

[8] Cf. Psa. 45:1; 46:1; 54:1 for similar notations.

Notes

Conclusion

The book of Habakkuk announces the just judgment which God would bring upon Judah by way of the Chaldeans, who would also be punished in due course. Habakkuk emphasizes the holiness and power of God, whose perfect faithfulness demands that His people maintain their trust in Him at all times.

Questions

1. How is the style of Habakkuk unique when compared to the other books of the Minor Prophets (Hab. 1:2-4, 12-17; 2:1)? _____

_____

2. What is the probable meaning of Habakkuk's name, and how might the meaning of the prophet's name be connected to the content of his message? _____

_____

3. Why is it likely that Habakkuk was written during the period of time after the death of King Josiah and before the Babylonian invasion of Judah (Hab. 1:2-11)? _____

_____

4. How would the information revealed to Habakkuk in the following passages provide comfort for the faithful remnant in Judah?

a. Hab. 1:2-11. _____

b. Hab. 2:5-20. _____

5. According to Habakkuk, how should the faithful respond when evil appears to triumph over good (Hab. 2:3-4, 20; 3:17-19)? _____

_____

6. How do the following passages of Habakkuk relate to Jesus Christ?

a. Hab. 2:4. _____

b. Hab. 2:14. _____

c. Hab. 3:13. _____

7. What questions does Habakkuk raise and how does God answer his questions?

a. Hab. 1:2-4, 5-11. _____

_____

b. Hab. 1:12-17; 2:2-20. _____

_____

Notes

8. How does Habakkuk describe the sins of Babylon in the following passages?

   a. Hab. 2:6-8. _____

   b. Hab. 2:9-11. _____

   c. Hab. 2:12-14. _____

   d. Hab. 2:15-17. _____

   e. Hab. 2:18-20. _____

9. In what ways does Habakkuk demonstrate the proper attitude of the faithful when it comes to placing one's trust in God (Hab. 3:17-19)?

   _____

   _____

10. What impact did the word of God have on Habakkuk, and why (Hab. 3:2, 16)? _____

   _____

Notes

Zephaniah

Notes

Introduction

Zephaniah is the thirty-sixth book of the Old Testament. The book of Zephaniah is generally recognized as the fourteenth of the seventeen Old Testament books of prophecy (Isaiah through Malachi), and is the ninth of the twelve books of the Minor Prophets (Hosea through Malachi). The theme of Zephaniah concerns the coming of God's judgment against both Judah (Zeph. 1:2-18) and the Gentile nations (2:4-15), which would prove His holiness and sovereign control of world affairs (1:14-17). The book of Zephaniah addresses the sins of God's covenant people (Zeph. 3:1-7) and calls upon them to repent in order to avoid receiving the full brunt of His wrath (2:1-3).

Origin of Zephaniah

1. Title. The book of Zephaniah is appropriately named for Zephaniah, the son of Cushi, the prophet of God, whose prophecies make up the content of the book (Zeph. 1:1). The prophet's name means "hidden by Jehovah," which is significant in light of the fact that his message offers the hope of being hidden from God's anger to those who repent and seek Him (Zeph. 2:1-3).[1]

2. Author. The opening statement of the book presents the claim that it contains the words which God delivered to the prophet Zephaniah (Zeph. 1:1). The book of Zephaniah is unique among the books of the Minor Prophets in that it provides an extensive genealogical background of the prophet, who is referred to as "the son of Cushi, the son of Gedaliah, the son of Amariah, the son of Hezekiah" (Zeph. 1:1). It is possible that Zephaniah's genealogy is meant to indicate that he was a great-great-grandson of King Hezekiah of Judah (Zeph. 1:1; 2 Kings 18-20), which would mean that the prophet was of royal blood and a descendant of King David.[2] Zephaniah was a citizen of the southern kingdom of Judah and was probably a resident of Jerusalem, since he refers to the city as "this place" (Zeph. 1:4), and prophesies from the perspective of one familiar with Jerusalem (1:10-11).[3] Since Zephaniah prophesied in the days of King Josiah of Judah (Zeph. 1:1), his work was contemporary with that of Jeremiah (Jer. 1:1-3), and probably Nahum and Habakkuk as well. Nothing is known of the prophet Zephaniah outside of the book that bears his name.

3. Date. Since Zephaniah prophesied during the days of King Josiah, the last good king of Judah who reigned from 640 to 609 B.C. (2 Kings 22:1-2), his message must have been delivered at some point during that

---

[1] Norman L. Geisler, *A Popular Survey of the Old Testament*, 257.

[2] Charles Dyer and Eugene Merrill, *Nelson's Old Testament Survey*, 807.

[3] Gleason L. Archer, *A Survey of Old Testament Introduction*, 394.

time.[4] However, it is evident that the book must have been written prior to the fall of Nineveh, since Zephaniah prophesies of that city's destruction, which took place in 612 B.C. (Zeph. 2:13-15).[5] Zephaniah also must have prophesied prior to the time of the religious reforms of Josiah (2 Kings 22-23) which began in 621 B.C., since he speaks of the rampant idolatry and corruption in Judah that would have carried over from the reigns of Manasseh and Amon (Zeph. 1:4-6; 3:1-4; cf. 2 Kings 21).[6] Therefore, it seems most likely that Zephaniah delivered his message sometime between 630 and 621 B.C.[7]

Purpose of Zephaniah

1. *Historical purpose.* The historical purpose of Zephaniah is to record the manner in which God warned the inhabitants of Judah of the impending judgment they would face for their rejection of God and His covenant (Zeph. 1:4-6, 10-18; 3:1-7) and emphasized true repentance as the only means of avoiding His wrath (2:1-3). The book of Zephaniah also provides the record of the specific judgments God would bring upon the various nations which surrounded Judah for their sins (Zeph. 2:4-15). However, Zephaniah would also offer hope by pointing forward to the time when a faithful remnant would return to serve the true God of heaven (Zeph. 3:8-20).

2. *Doctrinal purpose.* Zephaniah is intended to teach that, in spite of how things may appear, God is truly in control of all things and it is well within His power to punish the wicked (Zeph. 1:12-13, 14-17). The book also teaches that it is well within God's power for Him to triumph over false gods (Zeph. 1:4-6; 2:11) and to thoroughly judge, not only His own people, but the Gentile nations as well (1:2-3; 2:4-15). Additionally, the book of Zephaniah teaches that, though God is filled with wrath against the wicked (Zeph. 3:8), He is also righteous and faithful in keeping His promises (3:5), including His promises to restore a righteous remnant (3:9-13) and return the captives following their punishment (3:14-20).

3. *How does Zephaniah relate to Jesus Christ?* Since Christ is the overall theme of the Bible, the book of Zephaniah relates to Him in some important ways. In prophesying of a future in which people of all nations would worship the true God of heaven (Zeph. 2:11; 3:9-10), Zephaniah points to the time in which both Jew and Gentile would be brought together in one body through Christ (cf. Matt. 28:18-20; Gal. 3:26-28; Eph. 2:14-22). Zephaniah also speaks of a future in which the people of God would have the Lord in their midst as their King and Savior (Zeph. 3:14-17), which would ultimately be realized in the reign of Jesus Christ (cf. Matt. 1:18-21; Luke 1:31-33; John 18:36-37).

Content of Zephaniah

1. *Zephaniah describes the great day of the Lord.* In order to lead the wicked to repentance, the book emphasizes the impending arrival of

---

[4] Edward J. Young, *An Introduction to the Old Testament*, 199.

[5] Charles Dyer and Eugene Merrill, *Nelson's Old Testament Survey*, 807.

[6] Gleason L. Archer, *A Survey of Old Testament Introduction*, 394.

[7] Norman L. Geisler, *A Popular Survey of the Old Testament*, 257.

Notes

God's judgment as a day in which He would thoroughly punish the unrighteous. The prophet speaks of the "great day of the Lord" as a judgment which is "at hand" (Zeph. 1:7), "near" (1:14), and as a day which "hastens quickly" (1:14), rather than a judgment that is afar off. Zephaniah describes that day as a day of wrath, trouble, distress, devastation, desolation, darkness, gloominess, and alarm for those who have rebelled against the God of heaven (Zeph. 1:15-17). Furthermore, the day of the Lord would result in the devastation of both man and beast (Zeph. 1:2-3), would be a judgment which no amount of wealth would be able to deter (1:18), would culminate in the pouring out of God's wrath on all nations (3:8), and would be escaped only by a remnant (3:12-13). Zephaniah emphasizes the urgency of true repentance as the only hope of avoiding destruction in the day of the Lord (Zeph. 2:1-3).

2. Zephaniah condemns the sins of Judah. Much of the book addresses the wickedness of Judah and Jerusalem which would result in judgment and destruction. Zephaniah pronounces God's condemnation against the inhabitants of Judah for worshiping idols (Zeph. 1:4), for corrupting the worship of the true God by mixing it with the worship of false Gods (1:5), and for completely turning away from following the God of heaven (1:6). God's people would be punished for taking on the ways of foreign nations (Zeph. 1:8), for engaging in violence and deceit (1:9), and for complacently living as though God will neither reward the righteous nor punish the wicked (1:12-13). The prophet describes Jerusalem as a city which is rebellious, polluted by sin, and engaged in the oppression of her people (Zeph. 3:1), while at the same time refusing to be corrected by God (3:2), and whose thoroughly corrupt leaders consistently reject the law of God (3:3-4). While the just judgments of God which were witnessed by the inhabitants of Judah should have led them to repentance, they instead further corrupted themselves to the extent that severe punishment would be unavoidable (Zeph. 3:6-8).

3. Zephaniah pronounces judgment on the nations. While the book primarily addresses the sins of Judah and Jerusalem, Zephaniah also prophesies against the various nations surrounding Judah (Zeph. 2:4-15).[8] Philistia would be destroyed and left without any inhabitants (Zeph. 2:4-5), leaving that land to be occupied by the remnant of God's people who would return from captivity (1:6-7). Moab and Ammon, who had reviled and threatened God's covenant people (Zeph. 2:8), would be made as desolate as Sodom and Gomorrah, and would also be given to the remnant of Judah (2:9). Ethiopia would be slain by the sword (Zeph. 2:12). Assyria would be made as bare as the wilderness, and would become a place for wild animals to lodge (Zeph. 2:13-14), though Nineveh had been full of pride and self-importance (2:15). In bringing judgment upon the Gentile nations God would, in effect, be triumphing over the false gods in whom those nations trusted, thereby vindicating Himself as the only true and living God who is worthy of worship (Zeph. 2:11).

---

[8] "Zephaniah arranged the nations in a specific order to make his point. God would judge nations west and east, north and south of Judah (and everywhere in between). He would also judge nations that were near as well as nations that were far away. Those near would be plundered and possessed by Judah. Those far away would simply be destroyed by the Lord" (Charles Dyer and Eugene Merrill, *Nelson's Old Testament Survey*, 810-811).

4. Zephaniah may be divided into three sections. Following its introduction (Zeph. 1:1), the book falls into three main divisions, each serving a clear purpose in the delivery of the prophet's overall message. Zephaniah begins with a discussion of the day of the Lord (Zeph. 1:2-2:3), in which God will bring utter destruction upon the inhabitants of Judah and Jerusalem for their persistent idolatry and rejection of the true God (Zeph. 1:2-18), and closes the section with an appeal for repentance as the means of averting God's wrath (2:1-3). Zephaniah then continues his message by prophesying against the wicked pagan nations surrounding Judah, describing the severe judgments which God would bring upon each of them (2:4-9, 12-15) in order to demonstrate His sovereignty over all people (2:10-11). Zephaniah then pronounces a woe against the rebellious and sinful city of Jerusalem (Zeph. 3:1-7), and proceeds to bring the book to a close by announcing the coming deliverance of God in which a pure remnant will be saved (3:8-20).

Outline of Zephaniah

I. Judgment in the Day of the Lord (1:1-18).
   A. The judgment of God against Judah (1:1-13).
   B. The devastation of the great day of the Lord (1:14-18).

II. Repentance in the Day of the Lord (2:1-15).
   A. The call to repent (2:1-3).
   B. The judgment of God against the nations (2:4-15).

III. Salvation in the Day of the Lord (3:1-20).
   A. The woe against Jerusalem (3:1-8).
   B. The salvation of the remnant (3:9-20).

Conclusion

The book of Zephaniah announces the coming of the great day of the Lord during which God would bring His judgment upon Judah, as well as upon the Gentile nations. Zephaniah emphasizes both the judgment and deliverance of God, who would provide for the salvation of a faithful remnant of His people.

Questions

1. What is the meaning of Zephaniah's name, and how might the meaning of the prophet's name be connected to the content of his message (Zeph. 2:3)? _____

_____

2. How is the background information provided by Zephaniah unique, and what might be its significance (Zeph. 1:1)? _____

_____

3. Why is it likely that Zephaniah delivered his message prior to the religious reforms enacted by King Josiah (Zeph. 1:1, 4-6; 2 Kings 23:1-25)? _____

_____

Notes

4. According to Zephaniah, how had God's covenant people historically responded to His judgments (Zeph. 3:6-7)? _____

_____

5. How would the judgments announced by Zephaniah correct the thinking of the inhabitants of Judah (Zeph. 1:12-13, 14-17)? _____

_____

6. How would the following prophecies of Zephaniah be fulfilled in Jesus Christ?

   a. Zeph. 2:11; 3:9-10. _____

   b. Zeph. 3:14-17. _____

7. How does Zephaniah describe the judgment of the great day of the Lord in the following passages?

   a. Zeph. 1:7, 14. _____

   b. Zeph. 1:15. _____

   c. Zeph. 1:16. _____

   d. Zeph. 1:17. _____

   e. Zeph. 1:18. _____

   f. Zeph. 3:8. _____

8. For what sins would God punish Judah and Jerusalem according to the following passages?

   a. Zeph. 1:4-6. _____

   b. Zeph. 1:9. _____

   c. Zeph. 1:12-13. _____

   d. Zeph. 3:1. _____

   e. Zeph. 3:2. _____

   f. Zeph. 3:3-4. _____

9. What impact did God intend for His judgments against the nations to have on the Gentiles (Zeph. 2:11)? _____

_____

10. How would the final section of the book provide hope for those who would turn to God (Zeph. 3:9-20)? _____

_____

Haggai

Introduction

Haggai is the thirty-seventh book of the Old Testament. The book of Haggai is generally recognized as the fifteenth of the seventeen Old Testament books of prophecy (Isaiah through Malachi), and is the tenth of the twelve books of the Minor Prophets (Hosea through Malachi). Haggai is the first of the post-exilic prophets who delivered God's message to the remnant of the Jews who returned to Jerusalem following the period of the Babylonian captivity (Hag. 2:2).[1] The theme of Haggai concerns the urgency of rebuilding the temple following the completion of the seventy years of Babylonian captivity (Hag. 1:7-8).

Origin of Haggai

1. Title. The book of Haggai is appropriately named for Haggai the prophet of God, whose prophecies and work make up the content of the book (Hag. 1:1). The prophet's name means "festal," or "my feast."[2]

2. Author. The consistent claim of the book is that it contains the words of God which were given to the prophet Haggai so that he might deliver them to the leadership of the Jewish remnant (Hag. 1:1), as well as to all the people (2:1-2). The book specifically mentions Haggai by name nine times (Hag. 1:1, 3, 12, 13; 2:1, 10, 13, 14, 20) in connection with the prophet either receiving or delivering a message from God. Numerous times throughout the book the prophet credits his message to God (Hag. 1:1, 2, 5, 7, 8, 9, 12, 13; 2:1, 4, 6, 7, 8, 9, 10, 11, 14, 17, 20, 23) and specifically refers to himself as "the Lord's messenger" (1:13). Haggai worked together with the prophet Zechariah in order to prophesy to the Jewish remnant in Jerusalem following their return from Babylon (Ezra 5:1; 6:14). Almost nothing is known of Haggai's background, though it seems likely that he was born in Babylon during the exile and returned to his ancestral homeland with the group of captives led by Zerubbabel.[3]

3. Date. The book of Haggai contains the most precisely dated writings in the entire Old Testament.[4] Since Haggai dates his message according to "the second year of King Darius" (Hag. 1:1), his work took place in 520

Notes

---

[1] Following the decree of Cyrus (Ezra 1:1-4) in 539 B.C. which allowed the Jews to return to their homeland, a group of around 50,000 traveled to Jerusalem under the leadership of Zerubbabel the son of Shealtiel in order to rebuild the temple (Ezra 2:64-65).

[2] Charles Dyer and Eugene Merrill, *Nelson's Old Testament Survey*, 813.

[3] Edward J. Young, *An Introduction to the Old Testament*, 276.

[4] Norman L. Geisler, *A Popular Survey of the Old Testament*, 292.

B.C.[5, 6] Of the four messages of Haggai, the first was delivered on the first day of the sixth month (August-September) of 520 B.C. (Hag. 1:1), the second on the twenty-first day of the seventh month (September-October) of 520 B.C. (2:1), and the last two on the twenty-fourth day of the ninth month (November-December) of 520 B.C. (2:10, 20).[7] Therefore, all four of the messages of Haggai which make up the content of the book were delivered within a short period of time in the latter part of 520 B.C.

Purpose of Haggai

1. Historical purpose. The historical purpose of Haggai is to record the manner in which God rebuked the remnant of Judah for neglecting their responsibility to rebuild the temple (Hag. 1:1-11), and encouraged them to complete the task (1:12-15; 2:4-5).[8] The message of Haggai challenged both the leaders and the people to reorder their priorities in order to make the completion of the house of God their primary focus (Hag. 1:3-8). Haggai connected the lack of material blessings experienced by the restoration community with their lack of holiness and the neglect of their responsibilities toward God (Hag. 1:6, 9-11; 2:10-19). Additionally, the book of Haggai offered the returned exiles hope for the future with regard to the glory of God's house (Hag. 2:1-9), God's intent to bless His people (2:18-19), and God's control over the kingdoms of men for the purpose of fulfilling His promises (2:6-7, 20-23).

2. Doctrinal purpose. Haggai is intended to teach that, in spite of discouragement and distraction, the work and worship of God must never be neglected (Hag. 1:1-8). The book also teaches that God blesses and provides for those who make their service to Him their top priority in life (Hag. 1:12-13; 2:15-19; cf. Matt. 6:33). Additionally, the book emphasizes the need for holiness and purity in conduct (Hag. 2:10-14).

3. How does Haggai relate to Jesus Christ? Since Christ is the overall theme of the Bible, the book of Haggai relates to Him in some important ways. Haggai prophesies of a time when God would shake the kingdoms of the world (Hag. 2:6) and provide a glorious future for His house (2:7-9), which would be fulfilled in the establishment of the church of Christ (cf. Heb. 12:25-28; 3:1-6).[9] Haggai also speaks of Zerubbabel as God's "signet ring" (Hag. 2:20-23), thereby emphasizing God's plan to fulfill His promise to bring the Christ into the world through the royal line of Judah (2 Sam. 7:12-13; cf. Matt. 1:1-12; Luke 3:23-27).

[5] Edward J. Young, *An Introduction to the Old Testament*, 276.

[6] Darius I, also known as "Hystaspes" or "Darius the Great," ascended the throne of the Medo-Persian Empire in 522 B.C. (Gleason L. Archer, *A Survey of Old Testament Introduction*, 470).

[7] Norman L. Geisler, *A Popular Survey of the Old Testament*, 292.

[8] Though the foundation of the temple was laid shortly after the captives returned from Babylon (Ezra 3:8-13), the work ceased for almost sixteen years (4:22-23). The temple was finally completed in 516 B.C. (Ezra 6:15).

[9] Haggai's mention of the "desire of all nations" (Hag. 2:7) may refer to Jesus Christ, to whom people of all nations would come for salvation (cf. Isa. 2:1-4; Mic. 4:1-3; Mark 16:15-16), or it may refer to all that is desired and valued by the nations being brought into the house of God, thereby enhancing its glory (cf. Isa. 60:5, 7, 11).

Content of Haggai

1. Haggai contains four revelations given to the prophet. The book of Haggai is composed of four brief messages which God directed the prophet to deliver to the Jewish community of returned exiles in Jerusalem, led by Zerubbabel the son of Shealtiel and Joshua the son of Jehozadak, the high priest (Hag. 1:1). The first revelation given to Haggai, in which God rebukes the people for having neglected their duty to rebuild the temple (Hag. 1:1-2) while focusing on lavishly building their own houses (1:3-4), and failing to realize that God has withheld His blessings due to their disobedience (1:5-7, 9-11), motivates the people to obey the command to resume building the temple (1:8, 12-15). The second revelation given to Haggai is one in which God encourages the people, who may be discouraged by the inferior quality of this second temple when compared to the one built by Solomon (Hag. 2:1-4), by reminding them that God has always been faithful to his covenant (2:5) and would cause the future glory of His house to be greater than it had been in the past (2:6-9). The third revelation given to Haggai is one in which God rebukes the people for having lapsed in holiness and for having allowed themselves to become corrupted by evil influences (Hag. 2:10-14), while at the same time offering the promise of abundant blessings for those who would make correction and serve Him wholeheartedly (2:15-19). The fourth revelation given to Haggai is one in which God promises to shield Zerubbabel from the upheaval that He will bring upon the nations, thereby making him a symbol of hope for a blessed future for the people of God (Hag. 2:20-23).

2. Haggai focuses on the rebuilding of the temple. The emphasis of the prophet's message may be summed up in his direction for the Jewish remnant to build the temple in Jerusalem (Hag. 1:8).[10] Haggai's prophecy opens with a rebuke of the entire restoration community which had allowed the building of God's house to cease while they focused on the building of their own houses (Hag. 1:2-4, 9). The message of the prophet is so effective that, within a mere three weeks (cf. Hag. 1:1, 15), the people obey the command and once again begin working to rebuild the temple (1:12-15). Though the prophet's message anticipates disappointment and discouragement on the part of the older members of the community who would have remembered the vastly superior quality of the first temple (Hag. 2:1-3), Haggai offers the encouragement needed to complete the task (2:4) by emphasizing God's plans for the future, in which His house will be more glorious than ever (2:5-9). The completion of the temple, as the center of worship and representation of God's dwelling among His people, was vital to both the physical and spiritual wellbeing of the Jewish remnant (Hag. 1:8; 2:15-19).[11]

3. Haggai emphasizes the glory of the Lord's house. While encouraging the Jewish remnant to complete the task of rebuilding the temple,

---

[10] The first temple, which Solomon built, was destroyed by the Babylonian army in 586 B.C. (Norman L. Geisler, *A Popular Survey of the Old Testament*, 145).

[11] "It should also be understood that the second temple was to play a very important role in the history of redemption, for it was in this temple (as remodeled and beautified by Herod the Great) that the Lord Jesus Christ was to carry on His Jerusalem ministry" (Charles Dyer and Eugene Merrill, *Nelson's Old Testament Survey*, 813).

Notes

Haggai prophesies that God's temple will be filled with glory (Hag. 2:7), and that the glory of the Lord's temple in the future will far surpass the glory of Solomon's temple (2:9). Even though the physical and material splendor of the temple would never again match that of the first temple (Hag. 2:3), God would see to it that the future of His house would be far more glorious than its past (2:9) once He has shaken heaven, earth, and the nations in bringing about the fulfillment of His plans (2:6-7). Haggai's prophecy of the glory of the Lord's house (Hag. 2:6-9) would ultimately be fulfilled in the new covenant of Christ and the establishment of His church, or kingdom, which is the spiritual house of God, or temple (cf. Heb. 12:18-29; Eph. 2:19-22).[12]

4. Haggai speaks of the significance of Zerubbabel. The final message delivered by Haggai as recorded in the book is one that is directed to Zerubbabel (Hag. 2:21-23). Zerubbabel was a member of the royal line of King David (1 Chron. 3:17-19) who, as a descendant of King Jeconiah, was precluded by God from ever reigning himself as king (Jer. 22:24-30). Nevertheless, Zerubbabel was the leader of the first contingent of Jewish exiles who returned to Jerusalem following the Babylonian captivity (Ezra 2:1-2), and was made governor of Judah under the authority of the Medo-Persian Empire (Hag. 1:1, 14; 2:2, 21). Haggai delivers the promise of God that in the midst of the shaking of the nations that would take place as God worked to fulfill His great plans (Hag. 2:20-22), Zerubbabel would be considered God's "servant," "signet," and "chosen" (2:23). Haggai's message to Zerubbabel indicates that God would keep the promise He made to David concerning the fact that the Christ would come from His royal line (2 Sam. 7:12-13), and that Zerubbabel would serve as a key link in the unfolding chain of God's plan to bring the Savior into the world (cf. Matt. 1:12-13; Luke 3:27).

Outline of Haggai

I. Haggai's First Message (1:1-15).
  A. The Lord's rebuke (1:1-11).
  B. The people's obedience (1:12-15).

II. Haggai's Second Message (2:1-9).
  A. The encouragement of the builders (2:1-5).
  B. The future glory of the Lord's house (2:6-9).

III. Haggai's Third Message (2:10-19).
  A. The need for holiness (2:10-14).
  B. The blessings of obedience (2:15-19).

IV. Haggai's Fourth Message (2:20-23).
  A. The shaking of the nations (2:20-22).
  B. The messianic hope is preserved in Zerubbabel (2:23).

Conclusion

[12] "It must be obvious to a careful reader of this promise that the blessings which the Lord is here promising are spiritual in nature. It may be that this second Temple could never equal the first in material splendour and glory, but there was to come a glory far greater than that of the first, even a glory which would be brought about following a shaking of the heavens, the earth and the sea, and the dry land (cf. Heb. 12:26-28)" (Edward J. Young, *An Introduction to the Old Testament*, 277).

The book of Haggai contains the record of the encouragement God provided the Jewish remnant who returned from Babylon in their work of rebuilding the temple in Jerusalem. Haggai emphasizes the blessings God would bestow on His obedient people as well as a future in which the Lord's house would be more glorious than it had been at any previous time.

Questions

1. How does the manner in which Haggai presents his message support his claim to be "the Lord's messenger" (Hag. 1:13)? _____

_____

2. As far as the timing of the events is concerned, where does Haggai's message stand in relation to the destruction of the first temple and the completion of the second one (Hag. 1:1)? _____

_____

3. How is the work of Haggai as presented in the book of Haggai consistent with what is stated elsewhere in the Old Testament (Hag. 1:8; Ezra 5:1; 6:14)? _____

_____

4. According to the following passages, how was the obedience of the Jewish remnant connected to their material blessings?

   a. Hag. 1:6. _____

   b. Hag. 1:9-11. _____

   c. Hag. 2:15-19. _____

5. Why had the Jewish remnant neglected their responsibility to resume building the temple (Hag. 1:2, 4, 9)? _____

_____

6. Summarize each of the four messages delivered by Haggai:

   a. Hag. 1:1-15. _____

_____

   b. Hag. 2:1-9. _____

_____

   c. Hag. 2:10-19. _____

_____

   d. Hag. 2:20-23. _____

_____

Notes

7. Why might the older members of the restoration community be discouraged in building the new temple, and how would Haggai's message ease their disappointment (Hag. 2:1-9)? _____

_____

8. Why was the rebuilding of the temple in Jerusalem considered such a vital task for the Jewish remnant to complete (Hag. 1:8; 2:15-19)? ___

_____

9. How would Haggai's prophecy concerning the shaking of all things and the future glory of the Lord's house be fulfilled in the church (Hag. 2:6-9; Heb. 12:18-29; Eph. 2:19-22)? _____

_____

_____

10. Who is Zerubbabel, and why does Haggai emphasize his importance among all the members of the restoration community who had returned from Babylon (Hag. 2:20-23)? _____

_____

Zechariah

Introduction

Zechariah is the thirty-eighth book of the Old Testament. The book of Zechariah is generally recognized as the sixteenth of the seventeen Old Testament books of prophecy (Isaiah through Malachi), and is the eleventh of the twelve books of the Minor Prophets (Hosea through Malachi). Zechariah is the second of the post-exilic prophets who delivered God's message to the remnant of the Jews who returned to Jerusalem following the period of the Babylonian captivity (Zech. 8:11-12). The theme of Zechariah concerns the urgency of rebuilding the temple in Jerusalem (Zech. 4:9; 8:9). The book of Zechariah looks forward to the preservation of God's covenant people in the midst of the Gentile nations (Zech. 8:7-8), as well as to the ultimate fulfillment of their purpose in the coming of the Messiah and establishment of His kingdom (9:9-10).

Origin of Zechariah

1. Title. The book of Zechariah is appropriately named for Zechariah the prophet of God, whose prophecies and work make up the content of the book (Zech. 1:1). The prophet's name means "Jehovah has remembered," which is consistent with Zechariah's message that God has remembered His people and will bring His plans and promises concerning them to completion (Zech. 1:12-17).[1]

2. Author. The opening statement of the book presents the claim that it contains the words of God which were given to the prophet "Zechariah, the son of Berechiah, the son of Iddo" (Zech. 1:1), and this claim is repeated throughout the book (1:7; 4:8; 7:1, 8). Numerous times throughout the book the prophet credits his message to God (Zech. 1:1, 3, 4, 14, 16, 17; 2:8; 3:7; 6:12; 7:9; 8:2, 3, 4, 6, 7, 9, 14, 19, 20, 23; 11:4, 12:1). Zechariah worked together with the prophet Haggai in order to prophesy to the Jewish remnant in Jerusalem following their return from Babylon (Ezra 5:1; 6:14).[2] As a descendant of Iddo (Zech. 1:1), it appears evident that Zechariah was of a priestly family, since Iddo is mentioned among the priests who returned from Babylon under the leadership of Zerubbabel (cf. Neh. 12:1, 4, 16).

3. Date. Since Zechariah dates the starting point for the delivery of his message to the "eighth month of the second year of Darius" (Zech. 1:1), his work began in 520 B.C., just two months after Haggai the prophet be-

Notes

---

[1] Gleason L. Archer, *A Survey of Old Testament Introduction*, 470.

[2] Some have suggested that Zechariah was the younger of the two prophets based upon the reference to the "young man" within the book (Zech. 2:4). However, it is difficult to know for certain whether the young man spoken of here is the prophet, or the man in the prophet's vision.

gan to deliver his message (cf. Hag. 1:1).[3, 4] Zechariah's last dated prophecy in the book, which was given in the fourth year of Darius (Zech. 7:1), would have been delivered in 518 B.C.[5] Therefore, the dated prophecies of Zechariah (Zech. 1-8) were delivered within a two-year period from 520-518 B.C., while the latter part of the book (9-14) was likely completed by the prophet some years later, perhaps around 480 B.C.[6, 7]

Purpose of Zechariah

1. Historical purpose. The historical purpose of Zechariah is to record the manner in which God used the prophet's message to encourage the Jewish remnant to take seriously their task of rebuilding the temple in Jerusalem (Zech. 1:12-17), while offering assurance that the project would be completed (4:8-10).[8] The message of Zechariah would help the captives who returned from Babylon to understand that, if they would humbly obey God, then He would provide them with a glorious future (Zech. 1:3; 8:1-3, 9-23). Additionally, the book of Zechariah would offer the returned exiles hope for the future, in that while God would punish the Gentile nations (9:1-8), He would also preserve and bless His people (8:7-8; 9:11-10:12).

2. Doctrinal purpose. Zechariah is intended to teach that, in order to enjoy His blessings and promises, God's people must humbly submit to Him and obey His will (Zech. 1:2-4; 6:15; 8:14-17). The book also teaches that the Babylonian captivity came about as a direct result of the disobedience of God's covenant people (Zech. 1:5-6; 7:7-14). Additionally, the book emphasizes the sovereignty of God over the nations (Zech. 9:1-7) as well as His ability to bring to pass those things which He has promised (1:14-17; 2:10-13; 4:6-9).

3. How does Zechariah relate to Jesus Christ? Since Christ is the overall theme of the Bible, the book of Zechariah relates to Him in some important ways. The book of Zechariah portrays Christ as the "branch" (Zech. 3:8; 6:12) who would reign on His throne (6:13). Zechariah also speaks of Christ as the triumphant king (Zech. 9:9-10; cf. Matt. 21:1-9) who would be pierced (Zech. 12:10; cf. John 19:31-37), and as the Shepherd who would be struck while His sheep would be scattered (Zech. 13:7; cf. Matt. 26:31, 55-56).

[3] Charles Dyer and Eugene Merrill, *Nelson's Old Testament Survey*, 813.

[4] Darius I, also known as "Hystaspes" or "Darius the Great," ascended the throne of the Medo-Persian Empire in 522 B.C. (Gleason L. Archer, *A Survey of Old Testament Introduction*, 470).

[5] *Ibid.*, 472.

[6] *Ibid.*

[7] "Some have raised questions about the unity of the Book of Zechariah, charging that chapters 9-14 were written *before* the Babylonian exile. Linguistic differences do occur between the two sections of the book, and, as noted, chapters 9-14 are not dated. However, the linguistic differences can just as easily be explained by the different subject matter in the chapters and a different time of writing by the same author" (Charles Dyer and Eugene Merrill, *Nelson's Old Testament Survey*, 820).

[8] Though the foundation of the temple was laid shortly after the captives returned from Babylon (Ezra 3:8-13), the work ceased for almost sixteen years (4:22-23). The temple was finally completed in 516 B.C. (Ezra 6:15).

Content of Zechariah

1. Zechariah features an apocalyptic style. Much of the book of Zechariah consists of various symbolic visions which God causes the prophet to see and record (Zech. 1:8, 18; 2:1; 3:1; 4:1-2; 5:1; 6:1) and is filled with highly symbolic language (14:8-9) and acts (6:9-15; 11:10-17).[9, 10] Along these lines, the book begins with a series of eight symbolic visions through which God would convey His message to His people (Zech. 1:7-6:15), while the prophet is only occasionally called upon to deliver a straightforward message to them (Zech. 1:1-6; 7:1-7). The apocalyptic style of Zechariah includes a heavy emphasis on the use of angels to mediate God's message to the prophet (Zech. 1:14-17; 4:5-7) and to explain the significance of the visions which he sees (1:9, 19; 2:3-4; 4:1-2; 5:5; 6:4-5). The visions and symbolism employed by Zechariah would serve to captivate the imagination and hold the attention of those receiving his message so that God's will might be thoroughly communicated and impressed upon the minds of the hearers.

2. Zechariah contains eight visions. The first portion of the book consists of a series of visions which God caused Zechariah to see, along with the explanations of each vision in relation to the state of the Jewish remnant in the prophet's day (Zech. 1:7-6:15). The first vision presented to Zechariah is that of a man riding through the myrtle trees on a red horse, followed by three additional horses (Zech. 1:7-8), which is interpreted as symbolizing the all-encompassing knowledge of God as it relates to world affairs and His ability to bring His plans to completion (1:9-17). The second vision presented to Zechariah is that of four horns that have scattered Judah, Israel, and Jerusalem (Zech. 1:18-19), along with four craftsmen (1:20), which is interpreted as God's ability to defeat any nation which threatens to destroy His covenant people (1:21). The third vision presented to Zechariah is that of a man measuring Jerusalem with a measuring line (Zech. 2:1-2), which is interpreted as meaning that Jerusalem will be so heavily populated that walls will not be able to contain it (2:3-4, 6-13), however, God Himself would serve as the city's wall of protection (2:5). The fourth vision presented to Zechariah is that of Joshua the high priest being opposed by Satan while wearing filthy clothes (Zech. 3:1-3), and then having his filthy clothes replaced with clean garments (3:4-5), which is interpreted as God removing the sins of His people so that they can have a relationship with Him again (3:4-10). The fifth vision presented to Zechariah is that of a lampstand fueled by two olive trees (Zech. 4:1-3), which is interpreted as representing the power of God enabling Zerubbabel and Joshua to complete the task of rebuilding the temple (4:4-14). The sixth vision presented to Zechariah is that of a flying scroll (Zech. 5:1-2), which is interpreted as God's judgment overtaking the wicked in general,

---

[9] The Greek word *apokalupsis*, from which our English word "apocalypse" is derived, is defined as "a laying bare, making naked...a disclosure of trust, instruction, concerning things before unknown" (Joseph H. Thayer, *Greek-English Lexicon of the New Testament*, 62).

[10] The apocalyptic style of Zechariah is similar in many ways to that of Ezekiel and Daniel in that the book is comprised of symbolic visions and revelations. However, this should not be confused with the uninspired writings "apocalyptic literature" which was composed after the time of the prophets (Norman L. Geisler and William E. Nix, *A General Introduction to the Bible*, 263).

Notes

and thieves and liars in particular (5:3-4). The seventh vision presented to Zechariah is that of a woman in a basket covered by a lead disc being carried to Babylon (Zech. 5:5-11), which is interpreted as wickedness departing from the land of Israel (5:8, 10-11). The eighth vision presented to Zechariah is that of four chariots being pulled by horses (Zech. 6:1-3), which is interpreted as God's exercise of control over the nations for the purpose of establishing peace for His people (6:4-8).

3. Zechariah includes two burdens. In addition to the prophet's initial call for repentance among the returned exiles in Jerusalem (Zech. 1:1-6), and the messages which God delivered to His people through Zechariah (7:1-7, 8-14; 8:1-23), the book also includes two distinct prophetic burdens, or oracles (9:1; 12:1). The first burden includes prophecies against the surrounding nations, such as Syria (Zech. 9:1-2), Phoenicia (9:2-4), and Philistia (9:5-7), while promising God's future protection of the Jewish remnant (9:8, 11-17), along with the strength, freedom, and restoration He would provide (10:1-12), as well as the hope of the coming of Israel's everlasting King (9:9-10). However, the first burden also includes the warning that God will punish both those who oppress His people as well as His own people who reject Him (11:1-17). The second burden includes a prophecy of the survival of God's covenant people in the midst of hostile nations (Zech. 12:1-6) and the restoration of the royal house of King David (12:7-14) at which time forgiveness of sins would be made available to all (13:1-6) through the one described as a pierced son (12:10) and a stricken shepherd (13:7) who makes possible a relationship between God and His people (13:8-9). The second burden also declares that perilous times would lie ahead for the people of God (14:1-2), who would continue to have divine protection in the midst of their enemies (14:3-15), while the worship of their King would be the one universal religion to which all nations must give heed (14:16-21).[11]

4. Zechariah emphasizes messianic prophecy. Perhaps more vividly than any of the other books of the Minor Prophets, the book of Zechariah paints a clear picture of the coming Messiah, or Christ, who would reign as King over the people of God. Christ is described in Zechariah as God's servant, the "Branch," who would be foreshadowed in His work of building and ministering to the spiritual house of God by Zerubbabel, who would rebuild the physical temple of God (Zech. 3:8-10), and by Joshua, who would serve as the high priest of the rebuilt temple (6:12-13).[12] Zechariah further prophesies of the Christ as the triumphant King (Zech. 9:9; cf. Matt. 21:1-11), as the firstborn Son who would be pierced (Zech. 12:10; cf. John 19:17-18, 31-37), and as the good, but stricken shepherd, whose flock would be scattered (Zech. 13:7; cf. John 10:14-18; Matt. 26:31, 47-56). The book of Zechariah also contains the striking prophecy of the exact price that would be paid for the betrayal of the Christ (Zech. 11:12; cf. Matt. 26:14-16), as well as the purpose for which that money would

---

[11] These prophecies would be fulfilled in the gospel age in which Christ sits enthroned as King and all nations must come to Him for forgiveness and salvation (cf. Matt. 28:18-20; Mark 16:15-16; Acts 4:12; 1 Tim. 6:13-16).

[12] Zechariah's foreshadowing of Christ through Zerubbabel the governor and Joshua the high priest indicates that Christ would be both the ruler and high priest of His people (cf. Heb. 5:9-10; 8:1-2; Col. 1:13-14, 18).

eventually be used (Zech. 11:13; cf. Matt. 27:3-10). Zechariah's prophetic message closes with a view of the Christ enthroned as the everlasting King to whom all must submit and offer worship (Zech. 14:16-21; cf. Luke 1:30-33; 1 Cor. 15:20-25).

Outline of Zechariah

I. The Call to Repentance (1:1-6).

II. The Eight Visions (1:7-6:8).
   A. The rider and the horses (1:7-17).
   B. The four horns and four craftsmen (1:18-21).
   C. The man with the measuring line (2:1-13).
   D. The changing of the high priest's garments (3:1-10).
   E. The lampstand and the olive trees (4:1-14).
   F. The flying scroll (5:1-4).
   G. The woman in the basket (5:5-11).
   H. The four chariots (6:1-8).

III. The Crowning of Joshua (6:9-15).

IV. The Question Concerning Fasting (7:1-8:23).
   A. The call to sincere religion (7:1-14).
   B. The restoration of the people of God (8:1-23).

V. The Two Burdens (9:1-14:21).
   A. The first burden (9:1-11:17).
   F. The second burden (12:1-14:21).

Conclusion

The book of Zechariah contains the prophetic messages which God delivered to the Jewish remnant who returned from Babylon in order to encourage them in their work of rebuilding the temple in Jerusalem and in their faithfulness to Him. Zechariah emphasizes God's mindfulness and protection of His people, who could take comfort in looking forward to the glorious reign their everlasting King.

Questions

1. What is the meaning of Zechariah's name, and how might the meaning of the prophet's name be connected to the content of his message (Zech. 1:12-17)? _____

_____

2. What connection exists between the prophets Zechariah and Haggai, and how does Zechariah's message reflect this connection (Ezra 5:1; 6:14; Zech. 1:16; 4:9)? _____

_____

3. How would the message of Zechariah help motivate the Jewish remnant to take their responsibility of rebuilding the temple seriously (Zech. 1:12-17; 4:8-10)? _____

_____

Notes

4. How would the prophecies of Zechariah offer the faithful remnant hope in spite of their physical weakness compared to other nations (Zech. 9:1-8, 11-17)? _____

_____

5. What led to the Babylonian captivity of Judah, and why was it necessary for Zechariah to review this information with the Jewish remnant (Zech. 1:5-6; 7:1-14)? _____

_____

6. How do the following passages connect obedience to God's will with receiving blessings from God's hand?

   a. Zech. 1:2-4. _____

   b. Zech. 6:15. _____

   c. Zech. 8:14-17. _____

7. How would the highly-symbolic and visionary style of Zechariah compliment his straightforward message concerning the need to rebuild the temple? _____

_____

8. What is the point of each of the eight visions of Zechariah?

   a. Zech. 1:7-17. _____

   _____

   b. Zech. 1:18-21. _____

   _____

   c. Zech. 2:1-5. _____

   _____

   d. Zech. 3:1-10. _____

   _____

   e. Zech. 4:1-14. _____

   _____

   f. Zech. 5:1-4. _____

   _____

   g. Zech. 5:5-11. _____

   _____

   h. Zech. 6:1-8. _____

   _____

9. How would Zerubbabel the governor and Joshua the high priest foreshadow the position which the Christ would occupy (Zech. 3:8-10; 6:12-13)? _____

_____

_____

10. How would the following prophecies of Zechariah be specifically fulfilled in Jesus Christ?

a. Zech. 9:9. _____

b. Zech. 11:12-13. _____

c. Zech. 12:10. _____

d. Zech. 13:7. _____

e. Zech. 14:16-21. _____

Malachi

Introduction

Malachi is the thirty-ninth book of the Old Testament. The book of Malachi is generally recognized as the last of the seventeen Old Testament books of prophecy (Isaiah through Malachi), the last of the twelve books of the Minor Prophets (Hosea through Malachi), and the last book of the Old Testament. Malachi is the third of the post-exilic prophets who delivered God's message to the remnant of the Jews who returned to Jerusalem following the period of the Babylonian captivity (cf. Mal. 1:8). The theme of Malachi concerns the necessity of sincerity and holiness in the lives of those who would worship God at the rebuilt temple in Jerusalem (Mal. 1:9-11). The book of Malachi addresses the moral and spiritual decay of the Jewish remnant after the rebuilding of the temple (Mal. 1:6-8; 2:10-16), while looking forward to the ultimate fulfillment of their purpose in the coming of the Messiah (3:1).

Origin of Malachi

1. Title. The book of Malachi is named for the prophet whose message forms the content of the book (Mal. 1:1). The prophet's name means "my messenger," and is possibly an abbreviated form of a name meaning, "Messenger of Jehovah," which is appropriate in light of the fact that the prophet acts as God's messenger to the Jewish remnant, speaks of the proper role of the priest as God's "messenger" (Mal. 2:7), and prophesies concerning future messengers of God (3:1).[1]

2. Author. The opening statement of the book presents the claim that it contains the words of God which were delivered to Israel through "Malachi" (Mal. 1:1).[2] Numerous times throughout the book the prophet credits his message to God (Mal. 1:1, 2, 4, 6, 8, 9, 10, 11, 13, 14; 2:2, 4, 8, 16; 3:1, 5, 7, 10, 11, 12, 13, 17; 4:1, 3). Nothing is known of the prophet outside of the book that bears his name, however, Jesus and the New Testament writers quote authoritatively from his work (Matt. 11:10; Mark 1:2; Luke 7:27).

3. Date. Since Malachi writes of a time in which the temple has been rebuilt and sacrifices and offerings have been reinstated (Mal. 1:7-10; 3:8-10), his work must belong to the period following the return of the Jewish

---

[1] Gleason L. Archer, *A Survey of Old Testament Introduction*, 477.

[2] "Some have questioned whether the word 'Malachi' in Malachi 1:1 should be understood as a personal name or translated from the Hebrew as simply "my messenger" (as in 3:1). While both options are possible, on the whole it seems better to take 'Malachi' as a proper name in 1:1. All the other prophetic Old Testament books name their authors, and so one would expect 'Malachi' to be understood as a proper name" (Charles Dyer and Eugene Merrill, *Nelson's Old Testament Survey*, 833).

exiles from Babylon and sometime after the completion of the temple in 516 B.C.[3] Malachi refers to the leader of the land as the "governor" (Mal. 1:8), which would also indicate that his work took place in the restoration community of Jerusalem. It is interesting to note that the term employed by the prophet points to a Persian official, rather than to Nehemiah, who served as governor in Jerusalem starting in 445 B.C. and again sometime shortly after 433 B.C. (cf. Neh. 5:14; 13:6-7).[4] The sinful conditions of the inhabitants of Jerusalem described by Malachi are nearly identical to those that were corrected by Nehemiah during his second term as governor (cf. Mal. 1:6; Neh. 13:4-9; cf. Mal. 3:7-12; Neh. 13:10-13; cf. Mal. 2:10-16; Neh. 13:23-28). Therefore, it seems most likely that Malachi delivered his message at some point between the years 435 and 430 B.C. while Nehemiah was in the Persian capital prior to his second term as governor of Judah.[5]

Purpose of Malachi

1. Historical purpose. The historical purpose of Malachi is to record the manner in which God used the prophet's message to rebuke the Jewish remnant for their hypocritical worship (Mal. 1:6-8, 13-14) and moral decline (2:10-16) in the years following the rebuilding of the temple in Jerusalem. While describing the widespread corruption of the priesthood (Mal. 2:1-9) and the corrupt and disloyal attitude God's people harbored against Him even though He had demonstrated His love to them and had provided for them (1:2; 2:17; 3:13-15), Malachi's message would direct the Jewish remnant toward repentance (3:6-7). Additionally, the book of Malachi would offer the returned exiles motivation to serve God faithfully in the future by pointing to the judgment God would bring upon sinners (Mal. 4:1-3) as well as the blessings He would bestow on the faithful (1:11; 3:10-12, 16-18).

2. Doctrinal purpose. Malachi is intended to teach that, in order to render acceptable worship and service to God, His people must approach Him in sincerity of heart (Mal. 1:9-10), doctrinal purity (2:7-9), and personal holiness (2:17). The book also teaches that God is abundantly willing to shower His blessings upon those who humbly submit to His will (Mal. 3:7, 10-12; 4:2-3). Additionally, the book teaches that, while God hates sin (Mal. 2:16) and will not accept complacency in worship (1:12-13), He treasures those who are faithful (3:16-18).

3. How does Malachi relate to Jesus Christ? Since Christ is the overall theme of the Bible, the book of Malachi relates to Him in some important ways. The book of Malachi refers to Christ as the "Lord" who would come to His temple, serving as the "messenger" of God's covenant (Mal. 3:1; cf. Mark 1:14-15; Matt. 26:28; Heb. 8:6). Malachi also speaks of Christ metaphorically as a "refiner's fire" and "fuller's soap" who would refine and cleanse His people (Mal. 3:2-3; cf. Matt. 3:10-12), and as the "sun of righteousness" who would rise with "healing in his wings" (Mal. 4:2; cf. 2 Cor. 4:6; Acts 10:43).

---

[3] *Ibid.*

[4] Gleason L. Archer, *A Survey of Old Testament Introduction*, 479.

[5] Charles Dyer and Eugene Merrill, *Nelson's Old Testament Survey*, 833.

Content of Malachi

1. Malachi features a debate between God and His people. The majority of the book (Mal. 1:1-3:15) is made up of a series of questions and propositions set forth by God along with the objections of His people as Malachi is used as the messenger to convey the righteousness of God, while condemning the wickedness of his people.[6] In the course of the prophet's message the Jewish remnant is represented as interrupting God ten times by raising objections to what He has affirmed to be true (Mal. 1:2, 6, 7, 12, 13; 2:14, 17; 3:7, 8, 13). Throughout the book of Malachi God engages in debating six specific propositions with His people, including the questioning of God's love for His people (Mal. 1:2-5), the despising of God's name by His people (1:6-14), the callousness of the people toward God's marriage covenant (2:13-16), the questioning of God's justice (2:17-3:6), the rejection of God's laws (3:7-12), and the harshness of the words spoken by the people against their God (3:13-15). By engaging in a debate with His people by means of the prophet Malachi, God rebuked the Jewish remnant for their sinful actions and sought to correct their ungodly attitudes.

2. Malachi describes the sins of the restoration community. Though the Jewish remnant returned from Babylon and rebuilt the temple, Malachi points out that they have turned out to be no different from their forefathers with regard to their tendency toward rebellion and apostasy, both in religious service (Mal. 1:1-2:9), as well as in moral behavior (2:10-3:15). The sins of the Jewish remnant are described as including an ungrateful view of the love of God (Mal. 1:2-5), an irreverent approach to God in worship by offering refuse as sacrifices (1:6-14), a corrupt priesthood which leads the people astray and shows partiality in judgment (2:1-9), the divorcing of Israelite mates in order to marry foreign women (2:10-16), a lack of trust in the just judgment of God (2:17-3:3), social injustice and exploitation of the helpless (3:4-5), a consistent rejection of God's ordinances (3:6-7), a refusal to properly offer tithes (3:8-10), and the active discouragement of those who would serve God coupled with praise of the wicked (3:13-15).[7, 8] The restoration community to whom Malachi's message was delivered faced the clear decision of whether to repent and turn back to God (Mal. 3:7), or be consumed by the judgment of God (4:1). It is clear that Malachi's message met with some degree of success in leading at least a portion of the Jewish remnant to fear the Lord (Mal. 3:16-18).

---

[6] "His style is that of the scribes. It is known as the didactic-dialectic method, consisting first of an assertion or charge, then a fancied objection raised by his hearers, and finally the prophet's refutation of their objection. . . .This debating style is especially characteristic of Malachi" (James Orr, Ed., *The International Standard Bible Encyclopedia,* III: 1970).

[7] It should be noted that the sin of idolatry is not named among the sins of the restoration community.

[8] It is evident that Malachi prophesied during the same general period of time as that described in the book of Nehemiah in light of the fact that the sins of intermarriage with foreign wives (cf. Mal. 2:11-15; Neh. 13:23-27), neglect in paying tithes (cf. Mal. 3:8-10; Neh. 13:10-14), corruption of the priesthood (cf. Mal. 1:6-2:9; Neh. 13:7-9), and social injustice (cf. Mal. 3:5; Neh. 5:1-13) are described as the primary evils of the day in both books.

3. Malachi contains the Elijah prophecy. While Malachi prophesies of the coming of the Messiah as the Lord and messenger of God's covenant, he clearly indicates that another messenger would first appear on the scene in order to prepare the way for His coming (Mal. 3:1). As the book closes, Malachi records God's promise to send "Elijah the prophet" before the coming of the Lord (Mal. 4:5). As the messenger who would prepare the way for the coming of Christ, this "Elijah" would turn the hearts of God's people (Mal. 4:6). The New Testament identifies the fulfillment of the Elijah prophecy with the ministry of John the Baptizer (Luke 1:13-17), who preached repentance to the Jews in order to turn them to God and prepare them for Christ (Matt. 3:1-12; Mark 1:1-8; Luke 3:2-18), declared Jesus to be the "Lamb of God" (John 1:29-31), and refused to take any glory for himself (1:19-28; 3:22-36).[9]

4. Malachi emphasizes preparation in anticipation of the Messiah. It is fitting that the last book of the Old Testament would encourage the Jewish remnant to prepare their hearts and lives for the arrival of the Christ. Malachi assures the people of God that the Lord will come (Mal. 3:1), however, he also questions the ability of the people to endure His coming since only the righteous would truly be able to delight in His appearance on the scene (3:2-3).[10] In order to impress upon the Jewish remnant the need to spiritually prepare themselves for the coming of the Lord, Malachi closes with an exhortation for the people to keep the Law of Moses (Mal. 4:4) and look forward to the next prophet who would come into their midst, that is, the one like Elijah (4:5).[11] While Malachi offers one last exhortation in view of the coming of the Messiah, neglect of the prophet's final instruction would only lead to God striking the people with a curse (Mal. 4:6).

Outline of Malachi

I. God's Compassion for His People (1:1-5).
    A. The introduction (1:1).
    B. The doubting of God's love (1:2).
    C. The evidence of God's love (1:2-5).

II. God's Condemnation of the Sins of the Priests (1:6-2:9).
    A. The irreverence of the offerings (1:6-14).
    B. The failure to uphold the covenant (2:1-9).

III. God's Condemnation of the Sins of the People (2:10-3:15).
    A. The mixed marriages with foreigners (2:10-12).

---

[9] While it is true that John was not the Old Testament prophet Elijah in the literal sense (John 1:19-21), Jesus identified him as the one who fulfilled the prophecy recorded in the book of Malachi due to the nature of his character and work (Matt. 11:7-14; 17:10-13; cf. Mal. 3:1; 4:5-6).

[10] It is obvious that, though the Jews delighted themselves in the idea of the coming Messiah (Mal. 3:1), many did not delight in Him once He came due to their own sinfulness and unwillingness to repent when rebuked by Him (John 1:10-11; Matt. 23:1-36).

[11] Since Malachi is the last of the books of the Old Testament, his message would be the last word to the Jews of that era, who would need to spend the next four hundred years guided by the Old Testament Scriptures in the absence of any new prophetic utterance from God while awaiting the coming of Christ.

B. The toleration of divorce (2:13-16).
C. The approval of evil (2:17-3:7).
D. The withholding of tithes (3:8-12).
E. The harsh words spoken against God (3:13-15).

IV. God's Consolation for the Faithful (3:16-4:6).
    A. The remembrance of the righteous (3:16-18).
    B. The judgment of God upon the wicked (4:1).
    C. The healing of the righteous (4:2-3).
    D. The exhortation to follow the Law of Moses (4:4).
    E. The coming of Elijah to prepare the way for the Messiah (4:5-6).

Conclusion

The book of Malachi contains the stern rebuke delivered by God through His prophet to the restoration community which had digressed into a deplorably sinful condition following the rebuilding of the temple. Malachi represents the final prophetic word delivered to the Jewish remnant in anticipation of the coming of the Messiah.

Questions

1. What is the meaning of the name "Malachi," and how is the meaning of the prophet's name connected to the content of the book (Mal. 1:1; 2:7; 3:1)? _____

_____

2. How do the conditions described in the following passages indicate that Malachi delivered his message during the time of Nehemiah?

    a. Mal. 1:7-10; 3:8-10. _____

    b. Mal. 1:8. _____

3. How would the message of Malachi help motivate the Jewish remnant to repent and turn back to God in faithfulness (Mal. 3:10-12; 4:1-3)?

_____

_____

4. According to the following passages of Malachi, what does God require of those who approach Him in worship?

    a. Mal. 1:9-10. _____

    b. Mal. 2:7-9. _____

    c. Mal. 2:17. _____

5. How would the following prophecies of Malachi be fulfilled in Jesus Christ?

    a. Mal. 3:1. _____

    b. Mal. 3:2-3. _____

    c. Mal. 4:2. _____

6. What issues does God debate with His people throughout the book of Malachi?

a. Mal. 1:2. _____

b. Mal. 1:6. _____

c. Mal. 2:13-14. _____

d. Mal. 2:17. _____

e. Mal. 3:7. _____

f. Mal. 3:8. _____

g. Mal. 3:13-15. _____

7. How are the sins of the Jewish remnant recorded in the following passages of Malachi connected to the time period of Nehemiah?

a. Mal. 1:6-2:9; Neh. 13:7-9. _____

_____

b. Mal. 2:11-15; Neh. 13:23-27. _____

_____

c. Mal. 3:5; Neh. 5:1-13. _____

_____

d. Mal. 3:8-10; Neh. 13:10-14. _____

_____

8. How would Malachi's prophecy concerning "Elijah the prophet" be fulfilled in the ministry of John the Baptizer (Mal. 4:5-6; 3:1)? _____

_____

9. According to Malachi, why would the Jews find it difficult to endure the coming of the Messiah (Mal. 3:2-3)? _____

_____

_____

10. How would the final instruction given by Malachi help to prepare the people for the coming of the Messiah (Mal. 4:4-6)? _____

_____

Notes

Bibliography

Archer Jr., Gleason L. *A Survey of Old Testament Introduction.* Chicago: Moody Press, 1994.

Bauer, Walter, William F. Arndt, and F. Wilbur Gingrich. *A Greek-English Lexicon of the New Testament.* Chicago: University of Chicago Press, 1957.

Clarke, Adam. *A Commentary and Critical Notes*, Vol. II. Nashville: Abingdon Press.

Dyer, Charles and Eugene Merrill. *Nelson's Old Testament Survey.* Nashville: Thomas Nelson Publishers, 2001.

Geisler, Norman L. *A Popular Survey of the Old Testament.* Grand Rapids: Baker Academic, 1977.

Geisler, Norman L. and William E. Nix. *A General Introduction to the Bible.* Chicago: Moody Press, 1986.

Hailey, Homer. *A Commentary on Daniel—A Prophetic Message.* Las Vegas: Nevada Publications, 2001.

Hester, H. I. *The Heart of Hebrew History.* Nashville: Broadman Press, 1962.

Keil, C.F. and F. Delitzsch. *Commentary on the Old Testament,* Vol. 4. Peabody: Hendrickson Publishers, 1996.

McDowell, Josh. *The New Evidence that Demands a Verdict.* Nashville: Thomas Nelson Publishers, 1999.

Orr, James, ed. *The International Standard Bible Encyclopedia*, Vol. 3. Hendrickson Publishers, 1956.

Rawlinson, G. *The Pulpit Commentary*, Vol. 7. Peabody: Hendrickson Publishers.

Tenney, Merrill C., Gen. ed. *The Zondervan Pictorial Bible Dictionary.* Grand Rapids: Zondervan Publishing House, 1967.

Thayer, Joseph H. *Thayer's Greek-English Lexicon of the New Testament.* Peabody: Hendrickson Publishers, 1999.

The American Heritage Dictionary. Boston: Houghton Mifflin Co., 1985.

Vine, W.E. *Vine's Complete Expository Dictionary of Old and New Testament Words.* Nashville: Thomas Nelson Publishers, 1984.

Webster's English Dictionary. New Lanark: Geddes & Grosset, 2001.

Young, Edward J. *An Introduction to the Old Testament.* Grand Rapids: William B. Eerdmans Publishing Co., 1964.

CPSIA information can be obtained at www.ICGtesting.com
Printed in the USA
LVOW031742080812

293518LV00009B/21/P